BALTIMORE
CIVIL RIGHTS LEADER
Victorine Q. Adams

BALTIMORE
CIVIL RIGHTS LEADER
Victorine Q. Adams

THE POWER *of the* BALLOT

IDA E. JONES

FOREWORD BY LARRY S. GIBSON,
AUTHOR OF *Young Thurgood:
The Making of a Supreme Court Justice*

THE
History
PRESS

Published by The History Press
Charleston, SC
www.historypress.com

First published 2019

ISBN 9781467139939

Library of Congress Control Number: 2018959010

To schoolteachers who changed the world one mind at a time

CONTENTS

CONTENTS

FOREWORD

I last interviewed Victorine Adams on October 15, 2003. The two-hour interview was recorded in her apartment at Park Place in Baltimore. I began the interview by asking Adams to identify which of her many contributions she was most proud. Without the slightest hesitation, Adams said that she was most proud of her role in bringing a major U.S. Social Security Administration office building to West Baltimore, creating more than one thousand jobs in the city.

She then mentioned two other achievements. She spoke of the successful efforts in the early 1950s of her Colored Women's Democratic Committee that convinced the Baltimore City Board of School Commissioners to change the intended location for the construction of a new vocational high school for African American youngsters. The Carver Vocational High School had been slated to be constructed at Pennsylvania Avenue and Greenwillow Street, in an area called "The Bottom" and widely known as a red-light district. The school was ultimately built in a much more upscale area of the city near Easterwood Park. For the first time, a black high school in Baltimore had adjacent playing fields and green space.

The third achievement that Adams mentioned was her convincing the Baltimore city government to award the contract for the management of Baltimore's new Inner Harbor marina to a black businessman, Kenneth Wilson.

Later in the interview, Victorine Adams amended her list of proudest achievements by adding a fourth item. This was the successful effort in 1958 by her Woman Power organization in pressuring the downtown Baltimore hotels to begin accepting black customers, at least when connected to conventions and large meetings. She specifically mentioned the Hotel Emerson, the Lord Baltimore and the Belvedere.

As the interview progressed, I could not resist discussing her most enduring and visible product: the Fuel Fund Inc., which continues to provide energy assistance to Maryland families in need.

During those two precious hours, many more meaningful contributions emerged, most of which are chronicled in this excellent book by Dr. Ida Jones. This expertly researched piece of scholarship describes Adams's personal life and her remarkable career of leadership and service. The book also provides valuable insight into Baltimore and Maryland history.

I concluded our 2003 interview by asking Victorine Adams to make any concluding remark that she wished. She said:

> *This success that we enjoyed was not something that depended on one person. It was a united effort of many women who gave their time and their talent to the programs by which we were trying to move forward the community. These women also taught their children to help us get our program moving. I get a lot of credit for what many, many women have done. I want the people to know that I appreciate these women; I want to help other people to know about their contributions.*

Victorine Adams would be pleased that this book by Dr. Ida Jones does exactly that. It describes the vast range of citizens whom Victorine Adams inspired, motivated and led to improve the human condition.

Many of the key dates in Victorine Adams's fabulous career end in the number 8. She graduated from Baltimore's Frederick Douglass High School in 1928. She founded the Woman Power organization in 1958. She created the Fuel Fund in 1978.

We will all enjoy and be enlightened by this book for many years to come.

—Larry S. Gibson
Professor of law and author of
Young Thurgood: The Making of a Supreme Court Justice

PREFACE

I t is a known fact that the shortest distance between two points is a straight line. Human life is intersected by all kinds of lines. The most salient one is the dash between birth and death dates on a tombstone. For Victorine Adams, that line developed over ninety-three years. African Americans crossed lines of segregation to full citizenship, while women crossed lines from unfranchised persons to recognized voters during the course of Victorine's lifeline. The timing of her birth resulted in her living a life filled with awkward lines: racially restricted housing lines, gendered career lines, lined penmanship paper, dance lines, boutique dress hemlines and voter education lines. Many of those lines she sought to cross or eradicate during the course of her life to ensure that equality become the baseline for all Baltimoreans. In January 2006, there were two distinct lines winding through the streets of Baltimore: one a funeral procession for the late Victorine Quille Adams and the other at the Baltimore energy assistance office. The funeral procession for Mrs. Adams marked her passage from life to internment; from resident to historical personality. She succumbed to adenocarcinoma at the age of ninety-three. The other line was at the Baltimore energy assistance office connecting people in need with the necessary resource of fuel during the winter. During the course of her life, Adams innovated the Baltimore Gas and Electric Company's Fuel Fund. The Baltimore Fuel Fund provided economic assistance to residents who could not meet the costs of their utility bills during the winter. Ultimately, Adams's model

Fuel Fund was replicated by other cities across America to aid those in need. The *Baltimore Sun* reported on January 14, 2006:

> *Loretta Jennings was one of six city residents applying for help to pay utility bills, a subsidy program Adams pioneered over 25 years ago and that helped 31,000 people with their heat last year. But Jennings knew nothing of the local activist who strived humbly for such civic programs that propelled her, for a time, into the national political limelight. "It's funny how people go unnoticed who do such great things," Jennings said.*[1]

The two lines in January 2006 did not physically intersect; however, the woman and her vision intersected, and she continues to live on in the lives touched by financial assistance in many ways, from heating fuel to academic scholarships to political mentoring. Adams was like many African American women in Baltimore who provided leadership in civic, social, educational and political arenas on behalf of African American people in general and all marginalized residents. She accomplished this through her club work in the Colored Women's Democratic Campaign Committee and Woman Power, Incorporated, which she founded; the National Council of Negro Women of Greater Baltimore, in which she served as a charter member; and Sigma Gamma Rho Sorority Incorporated and numerous other organizations, through which she educated, organized, advocated and galvanized everyday housewives, mothers, schoolteachers and professional women into "an army that took to the streets seeking a better life through political power." So how could she "go unnoticed" after doing so much?

This work seeks to draw new lines out of and around the life contributions of Victorine Quille Adams. To many, she is most remembered as the wife of William L. "Little Willie" Adams, an infamous figure in Baltimore for operating a numbers-running business, as well as other enterprises. Historians make passing mention of her in areas of black women's club activity and Baltimore politics, but the only work solely examining her life is a graduate study, Kellian Kennedy's master's thesis, titled "Victorine Adams: The Civil Rights and Social Justice Movement in Baltimore," written at the University of Maryland–Baltimore County in 2012. Kennedy posits:

> [Adams] *is reflective of a multitude of women who buttressed the* [civil rights movement] *through behind-the-scene activism such as fundraising and voter registration. However, like many other women who worked with the Civil Rights Movement her activism was not limited to civil rights.*

Rather [she] *worked with a number of secular and religious groups to create equality, to provide resources for women and girls, and to assist people in poverty.*[2]

Kennedy does not intimate her reason for selecting Adams as the subject for her graduate work. She writes with insight from secondary sources positioning Adams at the center of all examination principally from 1946 to 1970. Kennedy draws lines between the civic activities of Adams and her spirituality. Integrating purpose and opportunity, Adams utilized her resources to make Baltimore a better place, a place of inclusion for all residents. Kennedy concluded, "Adams's biggest strength was she simply focused on the work, and let her actions speak for themselves."[3]

In 2012, six years after Adams's death, her personal papers were destined for Morgan State University's Beulah M. Davis Special Collections. Without an official archivist, the papers were maintained and organized by a small cadre of historians and volunteers. In 2017, the papers were processed and a finding aid was placed online. Within months, researchers trickled in to view the papers.

Prior to the processing of her archival collection, she remained within the deep lines of her imposing husband's personality. William "Little Willie" Adams's penchant for making money through bookmaking and illicit gambling still resonates throughout Baltimore circles in the wake of his death in 2011. Victorine was aware of her husband's industry and issued a strong opinion about it in the *Afro American* on December 25, 1971:

I am the wife of Willie Adams and his former status has been chronicled and presented for years and years. For fear that some uninformed people may think I occupy my City Council seat because—and only because—I am Willie's wife—I offer the following explanation. Whereas I am well known as the wife of Willie Adams—I am better known in my community as a diligent, hardworking civic worker and civic leader in my own right. I want to remind some, and inform others, that I carved a niche in Baltimore for myself with my teaching techniques by sheer dint of hard work. My husband's encouragement and financial support were not handicaps—but I did the purposing—the planning and saw to the execution of the many projects....I have paid my dues to Baltimore. I feel I should be regarded not only as the wife of Willie Adams but as a woman who has used her influence and affluence to better the community in which she lives.

She was a self-assured woman aware of the distortion that surrounded her race, gender and class in Baltimore. Yet and still, she managed to create two organizations, educate and register potential voters, hold politicians accountable to their constituency and maintain an impeccable reputation and social life. Adams wanted to make a difference in her community. At her funeral, Senator Barbara A. Mikulski told the mourners at St. Peter Claver Roman Catholic Church on North Fremont Avenue, "I learned [from Adams] about how to get things done....You really did change Baltimore. You really did change the world." She was an educator, organizer, civic leader, church worker, boutique proprietor, philanthropist, soror, mentor and wife. This is the Adams being presented in this work through the documents, photographs and printed materials she amassed over the course of her life. Through her archival collection, she leaves a blueprint for rising generations to live a life filled with compassionate conviction to inform the uninformed and speak for those who do not have a voice in the public arena.

ACKNOWLEDGEMENTS

Thank you to the following:

Victorine Adams for maintaining a comprehensive collection of materials that documented your life. Moreover, thank you for your foresight to deposit those items at your alma mater for future generations to learn from and about living a life of integrity and conviction with dignity.

William "Little Willie" Adams for ensuring those materials arrived at Morgan.

The Morgan librarians, historians and movers who received the collection of materials.

Mark R. Cheshire for writing about Willie Adams, presenting a man who loved and admired his wife of seventy-plus years and contributed to her humanitarian endeavors.

Larry Gibson for his support. His kind words and assistance in identifying persons in photographs were invaluable.

Beverly Carter for donating an original copy of Victorine's funeral program. This valuable document is now in her collection.

Joe Leizear, senior archivist at Maryland State Archives, for his superb reference assistance.

David Matchen of the University of Baltimore Law School Library for assisting me in answering the nagging question about the marriage bar and the Baltimore School Board.

Jenny Rensler of the University of Maryland Carey School of Law for articles about the marriage bar.

Emily Sachs of Enoch Pratt Library for combing through the public schools' directories.

Steven Ragsdale and the Baltimore City Historical Society for their dedication to excavating the city's history and historical actors in new ways.

The *Afro American* newspaper staff, past and present. Writing stories, keeping them and digitizing those ancient voices was an essential research tool.

Kate Weeks, whose persistent and mild nudging provided momentum needed to meet deadlines.

Arcadia Publishing/The History Press for seeing the value in sharing the story of a humble woman who desired to make where she lived a better place for all.

Finally, thank you to you, the reader, for taking the time to read this work. It is my hope that something about Victorine Adams will enrich your understanding of African American women in particular and some Christians in general who crusaded for justice in intimate ways, evoking change one person, one cause and one problem at a time.

Chapter 1

EVER SO HUMBLE,
THE QUILLE HOME

Victorine Adams was conceived at a time of tangled and blurry lines in Maryland and across America. The rise of domestic terrorism left mangled black bodies swaying from trees throughout the South. These gruesome spectacles were hoisted high to warn, threaten and proclaim the republic as a white man's country. Moreover, the political gains of the Reconstruction era melted away through the scalding white-hot heat of virulent racism and open violence toward African American politicians and citizens. In 1912, the year Victorine Adams was born, there were sixty-one African Americans lynched. She was born forty-seven years after the end of chattel slavery with the passage of the Emancipation Proclamation and sixteen after the United States Supreme Court decision in *Plessy v. Ferguson* declared the doctrine of separate but equal. Concurrently, she took her first breaths three years after the founding of the National Association for the Advancement of Colored People and eight years after Mary McLeod Bethune opened her school in Daytona Beach, Florida. The blurry line of African American citizenship gained greater focus in the twentieth century. Victorine's generation would be efficient stewards filled with race pride and impelled to action for the coming generation.

Yet, at the outset of the twentieth century, tangled lines of opportunity and oppression wove throughout Baltimore. The *Afro American Ledger* on November 16, 1907, reports on the returning state industrial fair:

> *For the first time in nineteen years the Afro Americans of this city and State will have an opportunity of showing what progress they have made*

Victorine as an infant. *Victorine Quille Adams papers, Box 12-14, folder 14. Courtesy of the Beulah M. Davis Special Collections, Morgan State University.*

during that time, when the Colored State Industrial Fair opens its doors in the Centre Market Hall on November 25....Here is an opportunity for our people to put on exhibitions, specimens of their skill and industry along all lines. There is ample room for a large display, and no one need fear that there will not be room for whatever they may desire to exhibit.... All Baltimore and the surrounding country should make it a point to pay at least one visit to the Fair during its continuance.

Fairs were popular mediums throughout the country where innovations, crafts and social and economic items were displayed. The colored industrial fairs, often associated with a Christian denominational affiliation, sparked opportunities for newly emancipated people to view the advancements made by members of their race. The state fair in Baltimore was under the direction of the Masonic fraternity. The *Afro American Ledger* thanked state officials from the governor to the mayor of Baltimore for allowing the use of the hall.

The zeitgeist of the era infused Victorine and those of her generation with a passion for education and equity. She and others did not view themselves as victims to injustice; they utilized their resources to provide for their communities and model examples for the youth. All of these accomplishments were obtained through orchestrated endeavors of collective work, dedicated leadership and a clearly defined goal of a better future. Victorine's family, church, education and profession composed the fuel she needed to plot a path toward that better future.

BALTIMORE, MARYLAND: GATEWAY TO THE SOUTH

The Baltimore of Victorine's childhood was a place of stark segregation. During the period leading up to the American Civil War, Baltimore's free black community was the largest in the country. Baltimore city was one of three main population centers of African Americans in Maryland. The state is bisected by the Chesapeake Bay; this famous estuary is also an ideological divide between the western and eastern shore. The agrarian economy of Maryland's Eastern Shore flourished—enriching the region's plantation owners and many of its small farmers—thanks to the export of tobacco and corn and the thankless work of enslaved Africans, who made up the lion's share of the workforce.

Baltimore city had its main industries of shipbuilding and ship maintenance, which attracted many African Americans, both free-born and enslaved. Baltimore was a small port town that employed skilled and semiskilled workers who served as caulkers, sailmakers, painters, carvers and common laborers. Many African American residents organized their communities into neighborhoods, fraternal orders, churches and benevolent societies. They established schools. Sharp Street Methodist Episcopal Church opened its first school in 1802. Sharp Street's congregation embraced the egalitarian vision of John and Charles Wesley and George Whitefield, the founders of Methodism, who promoted education in sacred and secular matters as essential to citizenship.

Historically, as Baltimore's black population increased, so did racial tensions. Baltimore's government could not accommodate the influx of needy blacks leaving the Eastern Shore and perhaps lacked the will to find a solution. There were few jobs available for the semiskilled or unskilled, and housing became increasingly difficult to find. In response, city officials criminalized African Americans for vagrancy and fined them for lingering on city streets. Often, the dismissal of African American needs placated working-class white residents/voters who could not leave the city and find racial haven in surrounding counties.

Employing the contrived stigma attached to black skin tacitly emboldened police, city officials and clergy who stoked the embers of racial antagonism. These moments were met by infuriated African American and radical white Christians. Both groups spoke out against the abuse black people suffered in Baltimore and sought to appeal to conscience and at times legal recourse to find a humane solution. Unfortunately, by the close of the 1870s and in the wake of a cholera epidemic in 1866, white Baltimoreans gradually separated themselves, leaving black Baltimoreans to fill small areas within the city. Yet and still, Baltimore was an attractive and ever-growing option for African Americans in other parts of Maryland. Concurrently, there were European and Russian Jews, Germans, Polish and other ethnic groups. Thus, a pattern was established in Baltimore that resigned African Americans to create within their own communities most everything they needed while working with accommodating white liberals and/or poor whites who had little clout or option to move away.

Mother, Father, Brother and Cousin Allen

A solitary thread of Baltimore runs through the life of Victorine Adams. Baltimore was her hometown and principal location for education from elementary to college, as well as the place where she served as a public school teacher and city councilwoman. Adams was the first-born child of Joseph Quille and Estelle Tate Quille. Married on Tuesday, November 21, 1911, Joseph and Estelle welcomed Victorine on Sunday, April 28, 1912, at Johns Hopkins Hospital. Her birth within six months of their marriage was no indicator of the depth of their marital bond. The Quilles had been married for thirty-three years when Estelle died on August 10, 1945. The cause of death was renal failure and complications from sickle cell anemia.

Left: Joseph C. Quille, Victorine's father. *Victorine Quille Adams papers, Box 12-14, folder 13. Courtesy of the Beulah M. Davis Special Collections, Morgan State University.*

Below: Estelle Tate Quille, Victorine's mother, standing near her fishpond. *Victorine Quille Adams papers, Box 12-14, folder 13. Courtesy of the Beulah M. Davis Special Collections, Morgan State University.*

Many working-class people had few options for employment; however, there were many jobs they could find to do in Baltimore. Joseph was a waiter, truck driver and barkeeper, while Estelle was a hairdresser and waitress. It is unclear how Joseph and Estelle met. According to the 1930 census, Joseph's parents were both Marylanders, while Estelle's parents were from Virginia. It is possible both Joseph and Estelle migrated to Baltimore as other African Americans did in search of better work, higher wages and seemingly easier living. Leaving behind the grueling, back-breaking work of tobacco plantations or produce farming in Virginia was an incentive for many Virginia transplants. Maryland natives living on the Eastern Shore worked in seaside occupations such as dredging for oysters or crabbing and were motivated to push out from the familiar, and Baltimore's industrial boon was a pull toward a better living. Moreover, the virulent racism within small pockets of Maryland and Virginia could spark moments of violence, resulting in loss of wages, property or one's life. Toward this end, many African Americans between 1870 and 1920 moved to Baltimore. Joseph and Estelle followed suit and found each other in Baltimore. Joseph, a single man of twenty-one, and Estelle, a single woman of eighteen, married on November 21, 1911. On April 28, 1912, Victorine's birth certificate listed the Quille residence at 1131 North Carey Street. Although Victorine was initially listed as Baby Quille, there is handwriting listing her full name as Victorine Elizabeth. A second child was born to the Quille union, William Career Quille, in 1913. Brother William worked as a delivery driver for Sadler Liquors. He served during World War II and the Korean Conflict in the U.S. Marine Corps. He helped organize the Imperial Detective Agency. He also worked for his brother-in-law at Little Willie's Inn as a bartender and at Club Casino as a manager. He married Tiara Harris, and they had one daughter, Linda Quille Wyatt.

Victorine's cousin Allen Quille, seven years her junior, later became an industrious business owner who "parlayed his bucket and rags into 17 parking garages."[4] Segregation impacted the lives of African Americans in obtaining loans and credit to open businesses. It restricted wholescale attempts to enter professional occupations that required apprenticeships in guilds. Therefore, those who attained an education, business or access to betterment often helped others, thus circulating the "black dollar within the black community," creating wealth and providing access. Allen Quille did such with his parking lot business. He started in high school, washing cars for $0.35 in the 1930s. Through hard work and thrift, he saved enough money to rent his first parking lot for $25.00 a month. He continued to

Left: Victorine and her brother, William "Billy," ages six and five. *Victorine Quille Adams papers, Box 12-14, folder 11. Courtesy of the Beulah M. Davis Special Collections, Morgan State University.*

Right: William "Billy" Quille, Victorine's brother. The picture's inscription reads, "To my darling sister with love. I still miss you both very much and I'm well and working hard I will write you soon. Cpl. Billy Quille." *Victorine Quille Adams papers, Box 12-14, folder 19. Courtesy of the Beulah M. Davis Special Collections, Morgan State University.*

reinvest his money, building an empire that yielded the city $3,600 a month in rent, in the same space where he worked as a teenager. His earliest parking structures were four- and five-story lots around North Charles Street, Hopkins Place, Lombard Street and St. Paul Street. By 1969, he operated a twelve-story garage on the Inner Harbor. It was a multimillion-dollar structure. By age fifty, he served as the president of the Baltimore Parking Lot Owners Association, which had over five hundred members. In a 1966 *Afro* article, Quille described himself as a "violent man" who fought the equality war "non-violently" from his pocket. He opted to "protest" in this fashion during the 1960s because he could not promise nonviolence on picket lines. In the *Afro*, reporter Bettye M. Moss quoted Quille as he remarked: "It's a wonderful thing. Certainly we need more of this type of constructive action. I feel it's a wonderful breakthrough.... This is the type of power we need. If others will take a look and use this as a yardstick it shows what can be done if you continue trying regardless of what obstacles or problems present themselves."[5]

Lastly, Allen Quille was charitable with his family and the larger community. He donated thousands of dollars to Gloria Richardson of the Cambridge, Maryland civil rights movement, as well as the Congress on Racial Equality. Locally, he donated funds to the Provident Hospital Development Program and served as the head of the Small Business Division, which eventually raised $50,000. He, too, had an interest in the youth and explained to them the benefits of hard work. His own story demonstrated the fruit of well-tilled ground.

THE COLORED CATHOLIC CHURCH: FREEDOM, SERVICE AND HUMILITY

Victorine's immediate family attended St. Peter's Claver Catholic Church. St. Peter's was founded in 1888 in west Baltimore by the Mill Hill fathers of Josephite Order principally for African American Catholics. The earliest sanctuary was in the Western Maryland Hotel on Pennsylvania Avenue, purchased by the Josephite fathers. St. Peter's Claver parish was the first of its kind for African Americans in west Baltimore. The congregation sprouted from St. Francis Xavier parish in east Baltimore. St. Francis Xavier is the oldest African American Catholic church in the country.

St. Francis Xavier was birthed in an era of revolutionary fervor. Uprisings in France and throughout its colonies shifted numbers of people. Many French nationals escaping the revolution and colonists escaping Toussaint L'Ouverture's insurrection came to America. They chose Maryland in part from knowing that Cecilius Calvert, the second Lord Baltimore, was given land in the New World between the Potomac River and the Chesapeake Bay. Calvert believed this opportunity was a way to grant persecuted Catholics reprieve from the Anglican Church of England. The religious tussle between Protestants and Catholics in England originated because of differing practices within the royal family. The state was named Maryland after Henrietta Maria, a Catholic English queen. The territory was settled in 1634. As immigrants arrived in the newly settled colonies, Catholics feared Protestant repression and passed the Maryland Act of Tolerance in

1649. The act ensured that religious freedom was available for all Christians in Maryland. Ultimately, the Protestants outnumbered the Catholics, and religious strife increased. Yet in Baltimore, Catholics and Protestants remained, and the Maryland Act of Tolerance contributed to the idea of freedom expressed in the First Amendment.

In view of the opportunity for religious freedom, roughly 1,500 white and black persons from Santo Domingo docked in Baltimore. These practicing Catholics resuscitated their faith in fashion and form throughout St. Francis Xavier. "Both groups were French-speaking, so it was logical that the San Domingans sought the spiritual ministrations of the priests, with whom they shared a common tongue. There the [San Domingans] Negroes found men willing to devote time to sacramental ministrations and catechetical instructions. Original catechetical instructions in July of 1796."[6]

The opening of St. Peter's sought to accommodate the ever-growing African American Catholic community while training select men for ministerial training. "On Sept. 9, 1888, the feast of the newly canonized St. Peter Claver, the Church of St. Peter Claver was dedicated by Cardinal James Gibbons. It was a great day for the black Catholics of west Baltimore. Preceding the dedication was a procession from St. Francis Xavier on the east side to the future St. Peter Claver on the west side."[7] Within four years, St. Peter's opened a school, the House of Good Shepherd on Calverton Street, and could boast a membership of 1,000 parishioners and 130 enrolled students. "Also in 1892, the fourth anniversary Mass was offered by the first African-American priest trained and ordained in the United States, Father Charles Uncles, S.S.J., a Baltimore native."[8] The early endeavors of St. Peter's established the congregation as one seeking social justice and called to social action through community service.

Unlike other cities along the Eastern Seaboard where large black populations existed, Baltimore hosted a historic Catholic community. Black Catholicism began with the founding of the Oblate Sisters of Providence. The Oblates were organized in Baltimore in 1828. "These pioneering sisters dedicated themselves as a Religious society of Coloured Women, established in Baltimore with the approbation of the Most Reverend Archbishop, who renounce the world to consecrate themselves to God, and to the Christian education of young girls of color."[9] The Oblate community refused to allow racial prejudice and derogatory gender discrimination to coward their sense of divine purpose and need within Baltimore. The co-founders—Sister Mary Elizabeth Lange, OSP, and Reverend James Hector Joubert, Society of Saint Sulpice (SS)—viewed the call to piety and service as a virtue available to black religious women. Lange's charisma, sense of spiritual duty and organizational skills established a foundation for the Oblates transcendent of imposed expectations from mainstream society as well as the larger Catholic Church. Born Elizabeth Lange in Santiago de Cuba in 1790, she lived and was educated in a French-speaking community. She left Cuba and settled in Baltimore, Maryland. Once she learned there was no school for black children, she opened a school in the Fells Point area with her friend Marie Magdaleine Balas. They operated the school for ten years. After co-founding the Oblate Sisters of Providence, she took the religious name Mary. Mother Lange died on February 3, 1882. Her legacy emboldened the Oblates, who continued in their mission to educate and evangelize African Americans. Historian Diane Morrow wrote:

> *Humility formed an essential component of the Oblate spiritual identity. In practice, the moral virtue of humility avoids inflation of one's worth or talents on the one hand, and avoids excessive devaluation of oneself on the other. Humility requires a dispassionate and honest appreciation of the self in relationship of the other to God. Embracing the religious state and rejecting secular concerns and status proved both liberating and empowering for these African American women. In renouncing the world to consecrate themselves to God, the Oblate Sisters inculcated into their communal consciousness positive senses of themselves as women of African descent. These empowering self-images prevailed for the Oblate membership over both the ambivalence toward them in the American Catholic Church and the disdain toward them demonstrated by white society.*[10]

To its credit and unique demographics, Baltimore city served as the first seat of the Roman Catholic Church in the United States. In the midst of enslavement, the Oblate Sisters of Providence were a contrasting image of blackness. It proved "anomalous to both the racial and religious orthodoxies" in nineteenth-century Baltimore, yet both institutions survived. "Baltimore sustained the Oblate Sisters because the city itself constituted an anomaly in southern slave society."[11] The Oblates contributed to the evolution of St. Frances Chapel, the earliest black parish in Baltimore. "By adding educational and social as well as spiritual dimensions to their lives through their church, the all-black St. Frances congregation countered the effects of the restrictions white society imposed on their existence."[12] They flourished throughout the 1870s and 1880s, maintaining free schools and an orphanage. By the 1900s, the Oblates provided shelter from the intermittent racial storms that denied the growing black population adequate education. These contributions came with a price of increasing debt to the Oblates, internal friction with the arrival of new leadership and fluctuating denominational interest. The perseverance of black Catholic women impacted the formation of Baltimore's Catholic community. Victorine's religious connection to Catholicism through St. Peter's Claver continued in an activist tradition that did not kowtow to racist pressure within the church or the city. Instead, she used wisdom, love and equity to bring about the beloved community described in scripture.

Moreover, her local parish, St. Peter's Claver, was aptly named for a Catholic priest who vowed to be "a slave of slaves forever." Father Claver's story begins in 1620 Cartagena, Colombia. Cartagena was a prosperous port trafficking in human chattel. Father Claver greeted each ship and stopped at nothing to feed, clothe, dress wounds, wash and assist in burying the dead among those persons. He used these moments of contact as missionary moments, sharing his faith with enslaved Africans. He also ministered to lepers, outcasts and other social pariah. His tenderness spawned hope in the downtrodden. He graduated from a Jesuit college in Barcelona and was beatified in 1850 by Pope Pius IX. His life demonstrated extraordinary heroic virtue and was worthy of universal honor. In 1896, Pope Leo gave him the official title "Patron of all Catholic Missions to the Negro" worldwide. The activism and humility of St. Peter Claver imbued Victorine with a servant's heart that resulted in a career in education and politics. Her lines of faith remained solidly Catholic until death. She did not accommodate the intermittent storms of racism within the Catholic Church; she worked with other blacks and liberal whites to rid the Catholic Church of discriminatory practices, as well as denounce those who used their pulpits to preach racist practices against blacks in Baltimore.

There were efforts throughout the twentieth century during which black Catholics openly confronted racism. At times, confrontations were negotiated into the formation of black parishes and congregations, while at other times there were direct action protests on behalf of marginalized groups. In 1925, the Federation of Colored Catholics (FCC), founded by Dr. Thomas Wyatt Turner, was a national organization composed of many involved African American Catholics who believed in the betterment of Catholic leadership. Dr. Turner was born on March 16, 1877, in Hughesville, Maryland, to Eli Turner and Linnie Gross, both former slaves. Denied admission to Catholic schools, he ended up at Episcopal schools for his formative education. From 1902 to 1912, he taught biology at the Colored

High and Training School in Baltimore. He was a charter member of the National Association for the Advancement of Colored People (NAACP) of Baltimore in 1909. He matriculated at Howard University, obtaining an AB degree in 1901. He obtained a PhD in plant physiology from Cornell University in 1921. Initially, he desired to attend Catholic University in Washington, D.C., but was denied admission on account of race. In 1917, he founded the Committee against the Extension of Race Prejudice in the Church, an early effort to highlight racism within the Catholic community.

Continued discrimination within the church and throughout the Catholic community resulted in the formation of another organization. Thus, "[t]he FCC's intent was to fight racism and segregation in the Catholic Church and promote racial harmony."[13] His parallel quest for inclusion sought to create access to higher education for "Negro Catholics" along the Eastern Seaboard. Unfortunately, the FCC was "forcibly" joined to the Catholic Interracial Council in 1933, after which it lost focus and momentum. Throughout his life, Dr. Turner published in the *Colored Harvest* and *Interracial Review* on issues of race and equity. He remained committed to his initial vision and continued to advocate for equality on behalf of black Catholics until his death in 1978.[14] This is an element of Victorine's Catholic heritage, as expressed by African Americans in Baltimore.

HOUSING, POLICING AND PROTESTING AS COLORED PEOPLE

Earl Lewis, of the Baltimore branch of the Urban League, described Baltimore as "not a northern city, strictly speaking, since it is below the historic Mason and Dixon line." However, there are times when Baltimoreans identify with southern culture. In examining the structure of industry in Baltimore city, the northern-like industrialism followed patterns in New England, while blacks migrating to the city found pools of southern areas from North/South Carolina and Virginia. The southern feel ebbed and flowed with the large number of blacks within Baltimore. Increasing numbers of blacks outpaced whites during the 1880s, 1920s and again in the 1930s. These surges in number swayed political, economic and social areas throughout the city. Housing, educating and employing swelling numbers of migrants strained opportunities for white immigrants from Europe. Logical moves to house blacks in segregated areas at times ran afoul of de jure ideals often backed by vacillating city, state and national government officials.

Despite attempts to expand beyond imposed racial boundaries, local or newly arriving blacks were "hemmed in by restrict[ive] covenants and neighborhood pacts" that were eventually codified by the city government in 1910. Baltimore mayor J. Barry Mahool signed into law an ordinance that provided for segregated/separate blocks for "white and colored races" to promote the general welfare of the city. Mayor Mahool understood that the pushback from white ethnic residents to an encroaching "Negro presence" would boil over into racial violence, as well as speculating from avaricious real estate salesmen. Lewis noted that the larger issue for city officials was a tenuous line between accommodating the growing black population within "contiguous areas" to avoid an impending race riot and utilizing the labor compensated at lower rates than white counterparts. Garrett Power informs readers that "Baltimore's segregation law was the first such law to be aimed at blacks in the United States, but was not the last."[15]

Both World War I and World War II brought a surge of migrants to work in wartime industry. Blacks were given the hazardous jobs for unskilled workers. These jobs, paying more than farming and offering economic improvement, pulled blacks from across the state and Eastern Seaboard. The Urban League and National Association for the Advancement of Colored People sought to acclimate new arrivals to city living. Expanding housing, offering social services and adequate schools all strained the limited resources the city and state offered black people. Thus, the black church and leading institutions contributed their resources. At times the government selected vacant lands to build housing for blacks or blacks would select vacant lands to construct their own housing, but both efforts were often squashed through civic disobedience or political maneuvering that would keep black residents contained within small areas that bulged, in part from friction within the community as a result of overcrowding, attracting police attention and surveillance. The police were leery of African Americans in general and therefore often exercised extreme force. Throughout the 1930s and 1940s, real or imagined criminal acts were brutally put down, often leaving severely injured black citizens.

Police violence marred relationships between the community and the city. In 1942, the killing of Private Thomas E. Broadus sparked a great outcry from the black community. There had been other killings; however, the killing of a former serviceman by a policeman over a dispute with a cab driver was unconscionable. It resulted in the formation of the Citizens Committee for

Justice, a collection of more than one hundred black organizations, from fraternal groups to religious denominations to civic-based entities. The Citizens Committee scheduled a march on Annapolis to bring attention to the abuse to the governor's doorstep. The keynote speaker was a Baptist minister from New York, Adam Clayton Powell. On May 2, 1942, the *Afro American* newspaper reported on African American outrage:

> *Some 1200 persons who crowded Sharp Street Methodist Church for the March on Annapolis mass meeting applauded Rev. A. Clayton Powell, told them: When you march on Annapolis, you're doing something history-making which will echo throughout the world because colored folks have said: "To hell with the world we are not going to stand this any longer.... There is a new Negro emerging today. Two years ago it would not have happened here in Baltimore but today we've had enough—we've gotten up nerve to [march] and we don't give a damn what happens. We believe it is better to die fighting for freedom than live a slave."*

The audience was a composite of black Baltimore—Protestants and Catholics, educated and working class, men, women and youth organized against unpunished criminal acts taken against black people. Juanita Mitchell Jackson, a director of the committee and member of the NAACP, offered to finance the trip. Organizers collected $500, ensuring that those wanting to attend could do so for free. Buses, cars and trains transported the nearly two thousand protestors to Annapolis. They were given an audience by Governor Herbert R. O'Connor, State Comptroller Millard Tawes and Secretary of State Thomas E. Jones. The committee demanded an end to discrimination in war industries in Maryland; investigations into police killings that had taken the lives of ten citizens in Baltimore from 1939 to 1942; and the appointment of colored uniformed policemen. In response to the demands, Governor O'Connor created a commission. Out of its fourteen members, only five were African American: Lucille Fitzgerald, board member of the YWCA; Edward S. Lewis, executive director of the Urban League; Lillie M. Jackson, president of Baltimore NAACP; Linwood Koger, attorney; and Bishop M.H. Davis of the African Methodist Episcopal Church. The commission was charged with studying the problems "affecting colored people" in Maryland.

In October 1943, the *Afro* reported that O'Connor was a "dignified, polite, self-defined friend of the colored people" who celebrated his record of placing three uniformed African American policemen in Baltimore. The results of World War II, O'Connor believed, would eliminate the concept of a "superior" race and launch an era of racial betterment. Yet he opposed the passage of a State Bill of Rights. In his opinion, it would "make people think that the Constitution was not enough" for all citizens. In brief, O'Connor indicated that Maryland is a "Southern State but not deep South" and would solve its own race problems over time. He believed his administration worked toward the goal of "fair play for the colored citizens," but he could not move too far ahead of the masses. *Afro* wrote that O'Connor quipped, "The teacher must not get the class mad by going too fast."

Young Lady, Student and Certified Teacher

The blurry and tangled lines of Victorine's infancy remained throughout her youth and young adulthood. Residents of Baltimore—the sixth-largest city in 1950, with the largest nonwhite population—had to employ legal measures to obtain basic civil rights. The top five—New York, Philadelphia, Los Angeles, Detroit and Chicago—had racial troubles but had come up with remedies to most city-based problems earlier. Los Angeles appointed its first African American police officer in 1889, while the African American officers in Baltimore were forced to wear civilian clothing, only receiving uniforms in the 1940s. Violet Hill Whyte, Baltimore's first African American policewoman, was appointed in 1939 and did not receive a promotion even after eleven years of commendable service and training two other female officers. From beaches to public transportation to lunch counter service, African Americans were denied service, and no recourse from the city or state sought to ameliorate those conditions. With a population of 900,000 residents, of whom 200,000 were African American, the *Afro* concluded that "the home of the 'Star Spangled Banner' should be ashamed of itself."

Education for African American children was the desired goal for the community. African Americans had a challenged history with education, both legally and logistically. Historically, enslaved persons had been denied formal education by law, which criminalized literacy. However, pre–Civil War blacks and philanthropic whites opened schools. The end of slavery flung open the doors to education. Victorine's generation benefited from the zeitgeist of nineteenth-century desires. It is no surprise that African Americans viewed education as an essential aspect of middle-class values. The Quilles were no exception. They believed in education. Both children attended public schools. Victorine attended Robert Brown Elliot #104 primary school. The building where Victorine attended school was located on Carey and School Streets. It was constructed in 1897 and designed as Colored School #9 by Mason Alfred Hawkins. Hawkins served Baltimore as one of several architects commissioned to draw up plans for various school buildings. The structure was intended to be a "three story plan with larger classrooms, wider corridors, indoor latrines, fireproof construction and at least one assembly room."[16] The school had many names: Colored School #9 (1897), Public School #112 (1901), Negro School #9 (1908–14) and Robert Brown Elliot #104 (1915 on). The series of 100s was created in the 1900s to separate African American schools from white schools. The Elliot school boasted the largest population of students in 1908; nearly 10 percent of the thirteen thousand African American students in Baltimore attended. The name of the school, Robert Brown Elliot, was selected to honor a man who was intellectually gifted and highly educated. Born in Liverpool, England, to West Indian parents in 1842, Elliot joined the British navy and arrived in Boston in the 1860s. In 1867, he moved to South Carolina, where his career blossomed. Ultimately, he worked as a newspaper editor and multilingual politician.

In examining the projected increase in enrollment, many other schools were in "poor shape," resulting in larger classes at better-equipped schools. The Elliot was given a score of 473 out of 1000. A score below 400 indicated that there were hazardous conditions affecting the safety, health and educational well-being of the students. The most glaring absence at Elliot was a playground. In 1992, the building was converted to elderly housing.

The topics taught at Elliot covered Negro history, nutrition, drama, poetry and recitation. Students participated in field trips to Western Maryland Dairy or Hendler's Ice Cream Factory. Many excursions stoked students to ask questions and learn more about food preparation and how industrial ideas and products came to market. Students were exposed to guest speakers, such as "race poet" Paul Laurence Dunbar. They were incentivized to write papers for classes, and at times, winning essays were published in the *Afro* newspaper. Victorine finished Elliot and matriculated to Frederick Douglass High School. Douglass High School was the only "colored" high school in Baltimore city. Initially opened in 1892 as a manual training program for boys with white instructors, it became the Colored High School in 1901, with black administrators and teachers. It was located in Victorine's neighborhood of West Baltimore. As it was the lone high school for black students, overcrowding pushed the administrators to offer two academic

Victorine teaching at Robert Brown Elliot, 1930s. *Victorine Quille Adams papers, Box 12-14, folder 11. Courtesy of the Beulah M. Davis Special Collections, Morgan State University.*

programs: one from 8.30 a.m. to 1:00 p.m. and a second session from 1:15 p.m. to 4:45 p.m. In 1937, the opening of Paul Laurence Dunbar High School alleviated the burden for students and teachers.

The material condition of the school was deplorable. Overcrowding and poor maintenance compounded matters. At the helm, Mason Albert Hawkins was the principal and was driven to ensure that his pupils obtained a quality education for themselves and for the race. Hawkins, a native of Charlotte, North Carolina, became the principal of Douglass High School in 1909. He attended Baltimore's segregated schools and earned a doctorate in 1930 from the University of Pennsylvania, writing his dissertation on Douglass High School. Hawkins taught German and Latin at Douglass and rose through the ranks to department head, vice principal and principal. His career of twenty-five years coincided with the improvement and move of the school into a million-dollar building on Carey and Baker Streets. During his tenure at Douglass, Hawkins spoke at various schools and colleges. He often wove in the need for race pride, history and achievement. In speaking

Victorine teaching at School #103 on Division Street. *Victorine Quille Adams papers, Box 12-14, folder 11. Courtesy of the Beulah M. Davis Special Collections, Morgan State University.*

at Cheyney Institute in 1915, Hawkins delineated the intention and impact racism had on the "Negro psyche" and self-esteem. The unrelenting battering on all fronts sought to destroy black people; however, "we" survived. Survival was a gift and responsibility of contemporary black people to ensure that the future would be brighter and better through the steps made in the present. The *Afro* reported Hawkins saying:

> *To this end there will and must result the development of the individual in mind and body; the strengthening of home life among us for the moral and intellectual conservation of our children, our most precious resource. We must maintain the high moral and religious sanction of our church life…an unfailing guide and comfort in our onward and upward struggle. And finally, there must be a continuous effort to obtain thru education and industry the knowledge and means for efficient individual and group life. Only thru the development of all social forces can our group become self-sufficient and play its part in the progress of the human civilization of the coming days.*[17]

The Hawkins years at Douglass challenged the students to become their best selves. The expectations and examples modeled served as viable encouragement for the students. Kate Sheppard, an English instructor at Douglass, worked in education for thirty years. She educated students in the primary level and eventually at the secondary level. Sheppard utilized her position as a teacher to place education at the center of each student's academic/lived experience. She started teaching in 1893 in rural Fairlee, Maryland. In 1923, she began teaching in Baltimore. Her notable pupils were Thurgood Marshall, the first African American Supreme Court justice;

and Juanita Jackson Mitchell, a lawyer and civil rights activist. Sheppard maintained an active life outside the classroom. She counted Mary McLeod Bethune, founder of the National Council of Negro Women (NCNW), among her personal friends. It was her friendship with Bethune that contributed to Sheppard aiding in organizing the Baltimore chapter of NCNW, of which Victorine was a charter member.

Victorine graduated from Douglass High School possibly in 1928. In that graduation year, there were no lists of graduates. Yet the *Afro* reported that Mayor Broening urged the students to "continue their pursuit for knowledge, but in seeking material things not to neglect their souls." Mayor Broening declared education was the safeguard of our civilization. The success of Baltimore's segregated and underfunded public schools produced competent students who left to attend the principal segregated high school.

The Baltimore Association, initially created to educate African Americans, realized there was a need to provide teachers for the growing segregated school system. Teaching was one of the four feminized professions, along with nursing, social work and librarianship. These careers were deemed nurturing fields that required a woman's innate ability to nurture. The desire for more African American teachers was a request of many black parents. The inspiration and expectation from black teachers would serve a dual purpose: it afforded students an opportunity to view their potential, while allowing students a sense of the familiar within the classroom. To the contrary, some black parents argued in an 1895 issue of the *Afro Ledger* that "it was perfectly satisfactory to have black teachers and separate schools, but if whites taught [blacks], then whites should have black teachers." That would never happen in staunchly segregated Baltimore; therefore, African American teachers were necessary to maintain the dual system.

Advocates including black teachers, mothers and Colored High School alumni worked to improve the existing schools through fundraising to obtain their goals. The issues were not simply aesthetics but also sanitation and safety. Tuberculosis and fire hazards were among the problems identified. Moreover, the inequity in pay for African American teachers versus their white counterparts resulted in protests throughout the state. According to historian Cynthia Neverdon-Morton in 1918, "The first-grade certificate qualified a white for at least $500 a year but for a black only $480 a year." Ultimately, after an injunction was filed in the Superior Court of Maryland, Baltimore had to equitize the pay for white and African American teachers. The feminized profession of teaching morphed for African American women in Baltimore into a position of organized activism. This line of activism remained a feature of black teachers. Victorine joined their ranks and followed that line of organized activism throughout her principal career as a teacher and secondary career as a civic activist.

The path to becoming a certified teacher followed the line of segregation. Coppin State University originally opened as a training school in 1900. The school provided the basic instruction for blacks in the state of Maryland. Since there was no interest in the white colleges to open their admissions to African Americans, in 1909, the pressure from the black community resulted in linking adequate teachers and the franchise together. The *Baltimore Advocate*, on February 13, 1909, reported, "In Maryland an amendment is pending to disfranchise colored men. If the colored men of the state organize and educate each other, the amendment will be killed and its advocates will hardly venture to make it an issue in this state again. Its death and burial will hasten the death of Jim Crow and disfranching laws."

African Americans understood the connection between government funding and education. The move to disfranchise "illiterate Negroes" sought to remove their ability to elect politicians who would serve the entire community, regardless of race. They knew that passage of the disfranchisement amendment would be the death knell of schools, businesses and employment. The amendment was defeated, and parents kept the pressure on demanding equity in all areas of life in Baltimore. In 1926, the Colored Teachers Training School was renamed Fannie Jackson Coppin Normal School. Fannie Jackson Coppin was born enslaved in Washington, D.C., in 1837. Over the course of her forty-year career, she obtained an education and advocated for the education of all, principally African Americans. In writing to Frederick Douglass about the purpose of education, Coppin stated, "This is the desire to see my race lifted out of the mire of ignorance, weakness and degradation....I want to see him... adorned with the enduring grace of intellectual attainments."

When Victorine enrolled in 1930, Coppin Normal School served as a two-year curriculum training African Americans interested in teaching elementary school. In 1931, the curriculum expanded to three years. Ultimately, the state board of education recognized the need for more elementary school teachers and recommended the curriculum and student population grow to meet the rising demand. Birthed out of a need, Coppin trained teachers to serve in a segregated school system with dignity. This provided generations of African American Marylanders access to teacher certification, placing them in classrooms where young minds were cultivated and thrived.

While teaching, Victorine enrolled at Morgan State College. Morgan, unlike Coppin, was opened by African American Methodist Episcopal ministers who sought to train future ministers. It opened in 1867 as Centenary Biblical Institute (CBI) to accomplish this goal. By the 1890s, women were admitted, and the name changed to Morgan College in honor of Reverend Lyttleton F. Morgan, a board member and fiscal backer. His large endowment provided an opportunity for CBI to offer collegiate courses. Victorine's matriculation at Morgan signaled a change in the racial balance within education. She entered during the presidency of Dr. John O. Spencer and graduated under the presidency of Dr. Dwight O.W. Holmes, the first African American president of Morgan. The shift from white to African American administration was a barometer of the growing talent pool of African American professionals.

Dr. Holmes was born in 1877 in Lewisburg, West Virginia, the son of Reverend John A. Holmes and Sarah B. Holmes. He spent his boyhood in New York, Maryland and Virginia as his father's pastorate relocated him. He attended Howard University and moved to Baltimore in 1902 to work at Douglass High School as a science teacher. He obtained an MA and PhD from Columbia in teacher training and higher education. His doctoral dissertation, "The Evolution of the Negro College," provided tangible evidence that race-specific schools were innovative, successful places that produced leadership in most every profession. His career in education spanned thirty-five years, and he experienced service in every position within the field, from teacher to registrar to dean and college president.

During his Morgan tenure, his administration orchestrated the transfer of Morgan from private to public ownership. Maryland allocated $350,000, of which $225,000 was used for salaries and improvement projects. On November 20, 1939, Morgan officially became a state college. Governor Herbert R. O'Connor appointed an interracial board of trustees to run Morgan College. In tandem with the transfer, Holmes prepared a ten-year "enrichment project," which he initiated to expand the campus offerings both intellectually and physically. One project included a new library. Although Maryland allowed for primary and secondary education, it neglected higher education for African Americans, and the development of Morgan was a way to amend that injustice. Once again, Victorine was exposed to the impactful aspect of education. Obtaining an education positioned the educator as an effective advocate and change agent. Her instructors, administrators and school namesakes all impelled and imbued her into the field of education with a sense of purpose and passion.

In 1940, Victorine's graduation year, tangled lines of racial antagonism plagued President Holmes. Hooper S. Miles, Maryland treasurer, referred to areas of Morgan's campus as "a rubbish heap of huts and shacks." Holmes responded that the campus was a work in progress and receiving minimal financial assistance from the state. Yes, there were shacks on campus—occupied relics from the farming era that remained on campus with tenants paying rent. In 1941, white neighbors resented Morgan's proximity since the school had moved to Hillen Road and Cold Spring in 1917. In 1941, Morris Macht of Welsh Construction Company proposed to build a brick wall and twenty garages along Hillen Road in front of the campus. The intention was to provide cars shelter from the elements; however, this construction would obscure the main entrance of campus, leaving a slender sidewalk for commuting students. Morgan lost the battle, and in May 1942, construction began on what Holmes dubbed the "spite wall," placing a tangible barrier between the town and the campus. In spite of drawbacks, Holmes persevered and grew the campus from 558

Victorine's graduation from Morgan State College, 1940. *Victorine Quille Adams papers, Box 12-14, folder 11. Courtesy of the Beulah M. Davis Special Collections, Morgan State University.*

students in 1939 to 973 in 1948. His example within Baltimore served Victorine well in preparing for her future as an educator both within and outside the classroom. The larger goal of equity was the greater aim for all Baltimoreans.

In June 1940, Victorine graduated summa cum laude from Morgan State College with a bachelor of science degree in education. Her class of sixty-two graduates contained twenty-six BA and thirty-six BS degree recipients. Four honorary degrees were awarded to Judge Jane Bolin of New York, first female judge in New York; George B. Murphy, Baltimore newspaper publisher; Eugene A. Clark of Washington, D.C., president of Miners Teachers College; and Harold Trigg of North Carolina, president of State Teachers College. Bolin and Murphy received honorary doctorates of law, while Clark and Trigg

Victorine as a young woman.
Victorine Quille Adams papers, Box 12-14, folder 14. Courtesy of the Beulah M. Davis Special Collections, Morgan State University.

received honorary doctorates of education. The commencement speaker, Dean William H. Hastie of the Howard University Law School, told the graduates:

> *In this present war, we have got to insist as never before that we're anxious to do our part but only if equal justice is meted out to us during this period [and] continuing afterwards. Now is the time for colored to say I am part of this country, proud of it, and believe in its destiny, but at the same time, this country must recognize me as one who must receive his share as well as give his share.…We can only hope that you can be vigilant, wise, open to and participating in public affairs in order to try to bring something out of this chaos and through our country bring a better and eventually happier life to the world of which all of us are a part.*

At the age of twenty-eight, Victorine Quille was a college graduate and certified teacher. The toxic segregation of Baltimore did not cower her spirit. Her connections at St. Peter's, Coppin and Morgan and among her neighborhood and family provided momentum that carried her into her thirties. The momentum fused race pride, civil rights and education into her ethos. The Negro spiritual "Don't Be a Weary Traveler," sung at her

Morgan commencement, fittingly states, "I look at de worl' and de worl' look new." The world was in fact new for Victorine. It was a new decade. The country was embroiled in World War II and women would find a new and larger space in wartime America. She was equipped to provide an income for herself with an upward trajectory. This was her time.

Chapter 2

TO HAVE AND TO HOLD

In Love, Work and Play for the Race

A ccording to Baltimore's Civil Rights Heritage website:

> *During the Great Depression, West Baltimore's "color line" had stabilized around Fulton Avenue. Beginning in the late 1940s, however, neighborhoods at the edge of Old West Baltimore began to transition from white to black. The change was driven by a number of factors including the rapid growth of Baltimore's African American population, the intense overcrowding and deteriorating housing conditions within historically segregated neighborhoods, and the movement of white households out of the center city to the suburbs.*

The containment of African Americans into specific neighborhoods remained a fixture throughout the early twentieth century. Pockets of neighborhoods were encircled abutting white ethnic and wealthy enclaves for fear of spreading violence, disease or visual displeasure. The city and state reinforced these boundaries through passing discriminatory laws or allowing unjust practices to remain in place.

EDUCATOR, ACTIVIST FULFILLING A NEED

The stifling reality did not impede Victorine or other schoolteachers. By 1900, 75 percent of American schoolteachers were women. Gender matters drove the women to demand pay equity and fair treatment. By the 1920s, pay and pensions were negotiated along with tenure regardless of gender. Women sought to occupy administrative offices, which men did not want to share. Men feared the effect of emasculation from women being in top administrative positions. Nevertheless, the women advocated and progressed forward with their demands, qualifications and desires. Unfortunately, the benefits of progress were not afforded to black schoolteachers. Underfunded, underpaid and segregated, black teachers protested and filed suit against offensive school districts to hasten change.

For example, Ida Cummings served as the first African American kindergarten teacher in Baltimore. A Morgan graduate, class of 1922, her teaching career started in 1901 after she passed the examination for city teachers. In 1919, she was the first woman elected to the Morgan Board of Trustees. Her tenure on the board spanned the campus's growth from Morgan College to Morgan State College, as well as serving with Dr. Holmes. She operated the Empty Stocking and Fresh Air Circle, which provided a vacation farm for impoverished children. The Fresh Air Circle was established by her mother, Eliza Jane Cummings, in 1912, and Ida continued to operate the vacation farm until her death in 1958. The example of Cummings modeled for Victorine the ever-present need for educators to nurture and cater to their students' whole experience. The teaching experience for Victorine included creating the School Marms. The Marms often traveled together. According to the *Afro* in June 1934, the School Marms held a jovial event where they "did romp" on a big scale. It was an evening of fun and games, with crayon-drawn pictures, lollipops and ice cream cone battles. The guests wore rompers, frilled knee frocks and baby dresses. This "kiddie party" offered clean fun.

The women kept one another company because in some states, marriage bars prevented schoolteachers from getting married. Once married, women were asked to leave. The bar implied that a woman could not teach full time and maintain a household because her principal duties would be to her husband and eventual family. Victorine worked as a student teacher in 1930 at School #112, where the principal was George B. Murphy and the vice principal was Estella W. Lee. Victorine remained in contact with Estella and returned to celebrate her retirement as principal from School #112 in 1958. Lee was eighty-one years old.

In July 1933, Victorine, along with twenty-five others, taught summer school at Morgan for 106 children in model classes; 81 of the students were housed on campus, while others were transported to and from campus. This model school sought to expose teachers to different methods of instruction while offering the students in grades one to six an opportunity to challenge themselves. The children selected were shown to have a high intelligence quotient, and their instruction would be by the best teachers in the system. The project was funded by the Public School Teachers Association and additional fundraising efforts. Included in the school program was a cruise on bay steamers. The courses were library methods, dramatic interpretation, English, history, mathematics, physics, chemistry, language, music, social sciences and psychology. In August 1934, the National Association of Teachers in Colored Schools held its meeting in Baltimore, and Victorine was in attendance. Attendees were welcomed at a reception held at Douglass High School where "a bevy of lovely schoolmarms served as hostesses." The organization comprised both male and female teachers and administrators. Over the course of the conference, speakers from lawyers to politicians to fraternal members addressed the "pedagogues." There were card games, with some thirty-five tables operating at one time, and prizes throughout the conference.

Victorine is listed in the Baltimore City Public School directory until 1944. Seemingly, she left the profession and sought another profession. In 1954, she completed a certificate in retail advertising copy from the New York University School of Retail. This later benefited her in operating the Charm Center and her political career.

Although busy with her profession, Victorine did not neglect her social life. She often went out to the movies, dinner and dancing. The idea of marriage was a desire for many girls in Victorine's era. The damsel rescued and the lone woman protected by a strong man were symbols of domesticity reinforced by Christian values. For African American women, marriage held a sacred space in the culture, emerging from enslavement and the brutality of labor that sought to scrub femininity from women while making brutes of men. Courtship, the delicate dance between prospective couples, involved all aspects of community, from home to church to neighborhood. *Who is he/she and who are his/her people?* The influx of migrants to Baltimore increased the pool of potential candidates, yet it resulted in greater scrutiny because of unknown persons without family or community ties to vouch for them. William Adams arrived in Baltimore, arriving at his uncle Reather's home. His mother's brother lived on the east side in a small apartment. William saw opportunity and wanted a life away from farming in North Carolina. Estelle, Victorine's mother, played the numbers and warmed to William through that association. Joseph, Victorine's father, was leery but came to like William over time and ultimately worked for him at Club Casino.

COURTING AND CONSIDERING MARRIAGE

Victorine's generation enjoyed socializing and had disposable income with which to party. Nightclubs and movie theaters offered entertainment and overall fun. Mark R. Cheshire, the biographer of William Adams, explains that Victorine and William met in an unusual way. William and associate Kenneth Bass were on their way to dinner in West Baltimore when they encountered Victorine. A benefit of segregation was the existence of concentrated public spaces where African Americans frequented and most everyone knew one another. The twenty-one-year-old Victorine patronized the same restaurant as William after watching a movie with an unappealing suitor at Harlem Theater. Her date wanted to extend the evening, but Victorine needed to get home in preparation for her class of first graders. She knew that if she did not work she would make no money, and her contributions to the household were anticipated income. Victorine was among the "most highly compensated" black teachers, earning $130 a month in the 1930s. The Depression slashed her father's income from $100 to $48 a month.

Toward the end of her dinner, a mutual friend introduced her to William Adams. Adams was a quiet person and left little impression on Victorine. Seemingly, something appealed to her—his good looks, quiet demeanor or rising reputation as a numbers runner. She agreed to a first date, which turned into a courtship and marriage. Their love affair surpassed the regional dispute in African American circles on the west side/east side debate. Residential segregation lumped all African Americans into densely packed neighborhoods. The Quilles lived on McCullough Street in the Sugar Hill district. Old West Baltimore was roughly 175 city blocks northwest of downtown Baltimore. The moniker Sugar Hill was borrowed from New York's Harlem. Baltimore's Sugar Hill attracted professionals and established working-class folks. Many of these residents, such as Victorine, would become leading figures in Baltimore through their accomplishments or contributing to the rising generation of successful professionals. In full view of legislated racial segregation, African Americans with means pushed farther west away from the east side. The residents of west side Sugar Hill were cohesive, and parenting instilled a sense of purpose in their children. The overcrowding and hardscrabble living on the east side widened the chasm between the rising "haves" and the perpetual "have-nots" in black Baltimore.

Willie lived on the east side with his uncle Reather. Uncle Reather's apartment was already crowded with his immediate family. Willie found work packing rags for shipment. The physicality of the job required stomping as many rags as possible into a shipping container. The overall environment was filthy and hazardous. The *Afro* reported in April 1928 that the east side is where "in the eyes of the whites they are just some more Negroes to be avoided and prohibited [while] in the eyes of Negroes, they do not live in Baltimore Proper." The article continued, "The two races live in the same blocks, where Negroes live in alleys and whites on the front streets." East siders worked with their hands as laborers. The *Afro* reported, "They do the dirty work and the heavy work; they carry out orders; they receive low wages; they feather the beds for vain white men and selfish blacks." The media painted an ugly portrait of east side residents. At times, the descriptions fit, while others were grotesque fiction lacking context. Nevertheless, this divide at times incorporated complexion differences; often, fair-skinned blacks lived and thrived on the west side and darker-skinned blacks occupied the east side. In looking at Victorine's parents, her father was a dark-skinned person, while her mother was a lighter brown. The issue of colorism within majority-black urban spaces frustrated people and chafed aspirations in all areas of social life.

Willie "admired" Victorine because of her exposure to higher education. Adams, naturally gifted with intelligence, did not have uninterrupted access to education; in North Carolina, colored schools were open only six months a year, compared to nine months a year for whites. Willie was raised by his grandparents, and the family income was based on laboring in the cotton fields of North Carolina. Willie's grandmother impressed on him to "learn how to count." She believed that once you mastered reading and counting, no one could take advantage of you. Adams took that instruction to heart and excelled in math at the local elementary school. Victorine's personal accomplishments and chosen profession melded with Adams's formula for black cultural improvement. According to Cheshire, "[Willie] was convinced that the way for Negroes to escape poverty was through creating and operating successful businesses," along with obtaining a solid education. Those twin aspects would elevate the race out of poverty. Adams arrived in Baltimore through his entrepreneurial efforts in collecting and selling scrap cotton, as well as refurbishing bicycles with parts he purchased with his scrap cotton money. Thrifty, intelligent and desiring a better life, Adams found numbers running an opportunity to make money to fund his larger business plans and ultimate desire to lift African Americans out of subsistent living.

As the two continued to keep company, Victorine's father, Joseph, wavered about this association, while her mother, Estelle, played the numbers. Victorine knew about what Adams did but did not press him for intricate details. Her parents' opinions did not impede her from seeing him. He continued to court Victorine with long-term intentions. On July 28, 1935, Victorine and William married at St. Peter's Claver Catholic Church. Their love affair was one of mutual race pride and socioeconomic justice. Those lines of love and justice strengthened throughout their seventy-plus-year marriage, morphing from a relationship between a couple to one that was focused on voter education, funding political campaigns, opening businesses, endowing scholarships and broad philanthropy. So just who was William "Little Willie" Adams, and what did he do to earn money?

Who Was William L. "Little Willie" Adams?

One cannot speak of Little Willie Adams without acknowledging his early activity in numbers running/illegal gambling. Born in poverty in the rural South and naturally intelligent, Willie desired a better life for himself and, ultimately, his people. This unique aspect of his persona is acknowledged in a few writings about his life; however, the larger infamy of his illegal gambling operation captivates the minds of most Baltimoreans. Mark R. Cheshire wrote *They Call Me Little Willie: The Life Story of William L. Adams* in 2016 to provide depth about him. Cheshire used personal interviews with Willie and Victorine, newspaper articles and court documents to recount the life of a numbers runner, prominent businessman and philanthropist of Baltimore. All proceeds from book sales go to the William L. and Victorine Q. Adams Foundation, "which generously supports education and other edifying endeavors in Baltimore." Cheshire's Little Willie is a transparent man with an innate gift for making money, employing people and empowering the African American community of Baltimore. His initial moneymaking effort in Baltimore was as a numbers runner. The runner was the lowest person in the gambling racket. Matthew Vaz explained that in numbers-running endeavors, the typical structure started with the banker at the top, the controller/branch manager, adders/back office bureaucracy and hundreds of runners working the streets collecting bets. Lastly, there were the pad/police protection. This illegal betting started in the 1920s in cities across the country. Many of these games were organized along racial lines and were contained within those communities. Vaz extracts the racial elements of illegal gambling, where black bankers sought to keep the money within the community. These men—and, at times,

Left: Willie as a young man. *Victorine Quille Adams papers, Box 12-14, folder 25. Courtesy of the Beulah M. Davis Special Collections, Morgan State University.*

Below: Left to right: unknown woman, pugilist Henry Morgan, songstress Billie Holiday, unknown couple and Willie Adams at Club Casino. *Victorine Quille Adams papers, Box 12-14, folder 26. Courtesy of the Beulah M. Davis Special Collections, Morgan State University.*

Muhammad Ali (*fourth from left*), Willie (*second from right*) and others, 1963. Carl X. Harden, photographer. *Victorine Quille Adams papers, Box 12-14, folder 26. Courtesy of the Beulah M. Davis Special Collections, Morgan State University.*

women—employed all strata of African Americans, and revenues were in the tens of millions of dollars. This business endeavor "filled a vacuum left by the failure of banks to service [black] need." This lucrative opportunity attracted organized crime and state legislators whose interests were solely financial. Within cities like Harlem and Chicago, the bankers were known as race men. These race men sought to improve the community through growing businesses and bringing financial opportunity to a neglected segment of the urban center. Thus, those men operated as "both cultural and economic institutions that played a direct role in financing [a black universe of] newspapers, politics, businesses, music and athletics." Willie fits squarely within this definition of a race man, and his public and private financial contributions align with that definition.

To the contrary, this idea of black economic self-sufficiency attracted white organized crime groups that sought to expand their territory into black economic spaces. The black numbers bankers did not cede territory easily, and in Baltimore, Willie seemingly fended off such speculators. In New York, white organized crime gained control, eliminating blacks from operational control. Moreover, they melded with police, creating a financial boon "at the expense of black numbers bankers." The unique position of Baltimore in the upper South afforded little opportunity for wholesale elimination of all black bankers, especially Willie. Shrewd, intelligent and desirous of other enterprises, Willie did not remain solely in the numbers racket. He expanded his holding to real estate, philanthropy, retail businesses, bars/nightclubs and manufacturing, thus sanitizing his operation while empowering others to pursue diverse endeavors.

In Baltimore, the State of Maryland took over the gambling industry. In 1973, Willie worked for the Maryland Lottery. He was hired as a consultant, in part from other state lotteries that failed to attract black gamblers, who opted to continue their own system of gambling. Vaz notes:

> *He clearly perceived that he had more to gain in welcoming the lottery than he did in reviving a public association with the illegal numbers. When the Maryland Lottery began its numbers game in 1976, his bars and liquor stores were among the earliest locations to receive lottery terminals for the new game. Willie was one of the few* [blacks] *positioned to access the profits of taxed gambling…and* [claimed he] *never spent a night in jail.*[18]

How Did He Become "Little Willie" Adams?

William Lloyd Adams was born on January 5, 1914, in Kings Mountain, North Carolina. The child of an interracial couple, he never knew his white father. The liaison between his mother, Claudia Black, and his father was one of power; she was his maid. Throughout history, domestic workers at times were exploited and abused. However, there is no definitive evidence to position Claudia as a victim. According to Cheshire, Willie's father was "a prominent businessman" who met him as an infant and "held his new born with pride." All of this he learned from Uncle Reather. Willie had a sister, Luvenia, born in 1911. Claudia left Willie and his sister with her parents in Zebulon, North Carolina, and traveled to Winston-Salem, North Carolina, to work in the cigarette industry. Willie was reared by his maternal grandparents, Ernest and Willie Adams.

His grandparents were sharecroppers. A sharecropper worked in farming and harvesting crops to sell. Often, these were unskilled laborers working on plantations that formerly enslaved themselves or family members. The relationship between the sharecropper and the landowner was economically abusive. The sharecropper had to pay for all of his needs from future profits and was always owing money to the landowner. This perpetual cycle of poverty re-enslaved generations of African Americans, tying them to the land. Willie's generation, on the East Coast, opted to abandon the arduous task of sharecropping, instead setting their sights on northern cities such as Washington, D.C., Baltimore, Philadelphia, New York and Boston. The factories and opportunities in northern cities promised a better life than the back-breaking poverty of sharecropping. The poverty in Zebulon was across color lines; whites were suffering as well. The children worked beside adults, men beside women, to meet financial obligations for their families. Willie was not spared any hard work because of his petite frame; he had to assist his grandfather to meet the needs of the small family of four.

Willie realized that poverty and lack of education were linked together, while offering a service created a stream of income. At about age ten, he picked up odd jobs to supplement the family income. With small hands, he dug deeper to harvest hard to reach cotton, which he sold three miles away from his hometown. Buyers were interested in his scrap cotton, earning him the nickname Cotton Field Willie. The money he earned he used to open a bicycle repair business. Many people in the rural South walked; however, bicycles were used by some to cover longer distances in a shorter period of time. This moneymaking opportunity allowed Willie to provide a service people were willing to pay for. Cheshire wrote, "Adams quickly emerged as the most reliable delivery boy in the area and consequently secured a steady stream of work."[19] In 1929, his grandmother died. Her death severed his ties to North Carolina, and he was free to move up north with his Uncle Reather in Baltimore.

In Baltimore, Willie was shocked by the open racism. White businesses overlooked black laborers; if they did hire blacks, they were under hyper scrutiny and subject to unfair treatment. Concurrently, a tuberculosis outbreak contributed to white flight and stronger boundaries between black and white neighborhoods. Willie went from stomping rags to working in a bicycle repair shop, but the financial devastation of the Great Depression resulted in unemployment. The twin conditions of racism and disease led Willie to think about returning to North Carolina—until he learned about the numbers racket. Uncle Reather's landlady asked Willie to read "a set of obscure numbers" buried in the local paper. If her numbers "hit," she would turn her one-cent bet into a six-dollar return. Willie queried, how did that work? The odds were against the backer of the bets unless there was a significantly larger number of losing bets than winning ones. Johnny Wiggins, his employer who operated the bike repair shop, also ran a numbers business from Fells Point. "Wiggins dutifully ushered him into the biggest numbers operation in East Baltimore, the Six and Eight Company."[20] The numbers business was illegal; however, the Six and Eight Company was "owned and operated by whites," therefore possibly avoiding inspection because of collusion between police and crime operators. Willie was able to convince Wiggins to vouch for him, and Wiggins guaranteed Willie's accuracy and efficiency from his work in the bicycle shop. The Six and Eight Company approved, and Willie entered the numbers racket as a runner.

According to Cheshire, the east side was not under control of one numbers boss; there were numerous bosses who controlled specific territory. There were tens of runners who could not poach customers, and they, too, had specific territories. Willie knew there was room to grow in this business, and he sought ways to innovate new customers and methods of collecting and paying out bets. His recent arrival and youth worked against finding new customers easily. However, his reputation of being punctual and reliable spread, growing his popularity. He used a bicycle to "cover more territory in less time" and reach untapped customers. Within one year, Willie sought to grow his 20 percent income as a runner to a larger share through subcontracting his low-level operation. "To qualify, a person needed three attributes: an established reputation for honesty and reliability, a strong command of mathematics and a genuine hunger to do more than earn a mere salary."[21] Willie understood at sixteen years old that character was an essential element of success only when coupled with comprehension and intelligence. If any of those three elements was missing, there would be a lack. His grandfather's hard work was undermined by his lack of comprehension, whereas an intelligent person lacking character would stagnate at one level. "He wanted people who shared his insatiable appetite for building successful business ventures, and not just for getting rich, although that was one of his many objectives."[22]

Willie was disgusted by the economic inequality that left blacks in perpetual poverty, in part from not owning businesses and sending their dollars out of the community to white businesses. If blacks owned their own businesses, the dollar would circulate throughout the community and benefit everyone, raising the standard of the overall community. He desired to make money and improve the condition of black lives. His businesses would treat customers, principally black people, the way he wanted to be treated. Within two years, he had purchased a candy store on East Eager

Street. At nineteen, he purchased a small barbershop. By twenty, Willie was an established operator throughout Baltimore. "His peers idolized him" and viewed his success as admirable. The higher he rose in the numbers racket and the more his business investments succeeded, the more the complexity of black economic success or failure to succeed became apparent. He noticed a troubling dilemma between squandering new income and possibly failing to obtain loans from white banks. There were numerous black-generated business ideas, and they did not lack the zeal in making the business work. However, "as the operation matured, more sophisticated and managerial skills were required," and few had such formal education or exposure to apprenticeships. Naturally gifted and inordinately frugal, Willie continued to hire sub-writers and purchase property and businesses. He moved from Uncle Reather's house into one he purchased for his sister, Luvenia, and her husband, which he gifted the young couple. As his popularity grew, so did his attention from young ladies. Willie did socialize and met a host of young women attracted to his looks and his money, but none would capture his heart until 1935. He also went to the movies with male friends, often business associates. In one 1931 production of *Little Caesar*, the story of a hardworking hustler determined to become the boss was a direct parallel of Willie's ambition. "After leaving the movie, [his friends] proposed the moniker 'Little Willie' and it stuck for life."[23] Willie worked on his larger vision in the numbers racket. He financed bets and sought to run a parallel business outside of his boss's knowing; if he were caught, the response would be unfavorable or potentially fatal. There was a period of panic when his side business infringed on his steady employment, but a white friend floated him a loan to replace the missing money, literally saving his life. According to Cheshire, Willie never identified the white friend; some speculate it was Irvin Kovens or Maurice L. Lipman. Willie and Irvin remained friends for over fifty years. The two men represented marginalized communities. By the 1930s, some Jewish residents had entered politics. Irvin hailed from an east side family. The *Baltimore Sun* reported in 1979 that "[Kovens and Adams's] relationship also developed into a political one, [while] complementing each other."

Born in 1918, Kovens grew up on the east side. Blacks and Jews were discriminated in all areas of life in Baltimore, forcing them to create a sense of community. Kovens started as a discount furniture salesman, ultimately becoming a political fundraiser. During the course of his rising political ambitions, he was convicted of mail fraud and racketeering, along with others, including former Maryland governor Marvin Mandel, in 1977.

He served several months of a three-year jail sentence. Kovens's political fundraising and power brokering positioned him as the most powerful man in Baltimore. His influence was greater than that of elected officials. Willie and Irvin remained publicly amicable and privately collaborated on business and political outcomes in Baltimore. Regardless, Willie surrounded himself with equally ambitious men who wielded power, operated businesses and sought to chart the future of Baltimore.

Willie was arrested, stood trial and testified before the U.S. Senate yet never went to jail. Concurrently, he lived his life as a wealthy man, funding numerous businesses, purchasing property throughout Maryland, donating to various causes, supporting aspiring politicians, fraternizing with professional athletes, desegregating Baltimore golf courses and employing numerous people. In 1977, he received an honorary doctorate from Morris Brown College. In speaking to the graduating class, Willie stressed the need to cultivate a good character: "I have been able in Baltimore to gain the confidence of the financial world by living up to my obligations, paying

Willie Adams (*left*) with unidentified people accepting trophy for Provident Hospital, 1970s. *Victorine Quille Adams papers, Box 12-14, folder 26. Courtesy of the Beulah M. Davis Special Collections, Morgan State University.*

Willie Adams presenting a check to Ida Murphy Peters of the *Afro American* newspaper. Peters was a daughter of newspaper publisher Carl Murphy. She orchestrated the "Clean Block" neighborhood contest, as well as the Mrs. Santa charity drive that provided for needy families during the holidays. *Victorine Quille Adams papers, Box 12-14, folder 26. Courtesy of the Beulah M. Davis Special Collections, Morgan State University.*

all bills when due, and keeping my promises. This was done with honesty, integrity, and ethical conduct in all of my lines of businesses at all times. We must integrate our businesses if we want to grow."[24]

With a seventh-grade education, Willie continued to challenge himself by taking additional classes and surrounding himself with educated people. He delineated that the aspects of a good character included hard work, education, interracial cooperation and philanthropy. Those elements were successful in his business model, and he imparted that to the graduates.

BECOMING MRS. WILLIE ADAMS

Victorine and Willie were a handsome couple. They lived in an apartment above Little Willie's Inn, a tavern. Victorine's father, Joseph Quille, was the club manager. In June 1938, Victorine and Willie were awakened when a bomb exploded in front of the tavern. The police alleged that organized crime ordered the bombing to drive Willie out of the numbers racket. Willie asserted that the bombing was racially motivated and not a criminal shakedown. On June 25, 1938, the *Afro* reported that Adams brushed aside underworld theories and accused Julius Fink. Willie asserted that Fink "ordered him to kick in with 5 per cent of the earnings of his prosperous tavern." Fink and his associate informed Willie he would have to "kick in" to protect his business. Joseph testified that Fink came to the tavern looking for Willie on several occasions. Victorine suffered nervous shock as a result of the bombing, and other residents of the building were mildly injured, but no lives were lost. Fink was charged with assault with intent to kill. Willie clung to the belief that the bombing was racial hatred inspired by jealousy because of the tavern's success. The article ran with a picture of Victorine alone, with the caption "Mrs. Victorine Quille Adams, who with her husband, Little Willie Adams, Baltimore tavern keeper, was in their upstairs apartment when white racketeers bombed their place." The visual with the article displayed an element of respectability for Willie. Victorine was a schoolteacher whose profession placed her within an elite class for black women. The academic accomplishments needed, the steady employment and respect they garnered elevated Willie to middle-class status, above a two-bit criminal. Victorine and Willie would employ their unique stature throughout Baltimore, sanitizing his reputation while positioning her as a dutiful wife and humanitarian.

The divergent paths that brought Victorine and Willie to adulthood converged when issues of youth, race and opportunity were concerned. Willie offered employment to most men in all of his businesses. He empowered them through offering employees partial ownership, thereby paying themselves while he took a percentage. This method worked to ensure that employees were loyal and learned skills that they could grow into other endeavors, at times financially backed by Willie, whose reputation brought customers. Victorine would come to meet Henry Parks, Lloyd Randolph, Marvin Mandel and Joe Louis through Willie. The aims of business, politics and philanthropy resided in most of Willie's friends. Within their first ten years of marriage, these ideas appealed to Victorine, nudging her to leave the

Willie and Victorine. *Victorine Quille Adams papers, Box 12-14, folder 23. Courtesy of the Beulah M. Davis Special Collections, Morgan State University.*

classroom to challenge the general misinformation about voter registration among African Americans in Baltimore.

She met Henry Parks through Willie. He became a mutual friend of the Adamses and a political colleague of Victorine's. Parks was born in Atlanta, Georgia, in 1916. His family relocated to Ohio, where he was educated and worked in a variety of companies. He obtained a BS degree in marketing from the Ohio State University in 1934. His career spanned sales and co-ownerships of regional and national brand name products. Henry's public relations firm was retained by boxer Joe Louis to market his wife Marva's singing career. Unfortunately, Marva did not have a marketable singing voice, yet Joe invested in her dream. Nevertheless, Henry served as her road manager, and that is how he serendipitously met Willie. Henry was a wizard in racial marketing. His proposal to extend Pabst beer into the black community was genius: use a celebrity to attract black dollars, and they would buy the product. Willie, enamored by Henry's education and drive, quickly named him a business partner. Their relationship and exploits stretched from Baltimore to Cleveland, Ohio.

Willie received business proposals of all kinds. One proposal from Ohio piqued his interest. Henry's proposal would salvage a struggling business, relaunching a quality sausage product. Henry's education and experience were an answered prayer to Willie's desire to leave the numbers racket. In 1951, Henry desired his own business. Willie provided the needed capital of $60,000. He also "gave" the operational interest to Henry. Willie's partnership remained shadowed, while Henry became the public face of Parks Sausages. Similar to others, Henry wanted to distance himself from Willie's illegal activities in the public eye through promoting a spotless image. Moreover, white market forces could destroy fledgling black businesses. Henry offered white stores the advantage to simply provide space for the product without any financial investment, and if the product did not sell, his men would collect the remaining product without any loss for no sales. "By 1968, 75 percent of the H.G. Parks, Inc. market was white. New York sold more of his products than Baltimore. Henry [and company laughed at the story of a meat buyer who said, 'I am not interested in nigger sausage']. Henry replied, 'I am not trying to sell you one. So now let's talk business.' Henry made the sale."[25]

In 1968, Safeway stores in the mid-Atlantic region opened their shelves to Parks Sausages. Safeway was the first national chain store to open to Parks. Safeway's endorsement propelled Parks Sausages into a huge success. "[Henry] captured the attention of corporate America."[26] By the 1970s, H.G. Parks, Inc. grossed $12 million a year. In Maryland, Parks Sausages attracted the attention of the U.S. military. Parks products were sold on numerous military bases throughout the region. Similar to Willie, Henry utilized his economic power to be philanthropic, as well as garner political power. He was elected to the Baltimore City Council in 1963, Goucher College Board of Trustees in 1969 and Provident Hospital Board of Trustees in 1970. Henry's business supported numerous activities sponsored by Victorine's clubs. Often pictured together, Henry and Victorine worked in local politics and campaigned together in the 1960s.

Another mutual friend of the Adams family was Lloyd Randolph. He, too, would become a political colleague of Victorine's. Randolph was born in 1905 in Keyser, West Virginia. He came to Baltimore as a child. He attended Douglass High School and served as the first black chief clerk of the city board of elections. Prior to entering politics, Randolph worked as a hotelier at a location where Negro League players came to stay in the age of segregation. Throughout the 1940s, Randolph's hotel served as a meeting place for voter education. A longtime Democrat, he was appointed to the Maryland House of Delegates in 1968. The *Baltimore Sun* reported that Victorine credited him with interesting her and Willie in politics in the 1940s. The *Sun* stated, "Eventually, it was the Adams family's political influence in West Baltimore that brought Mr. Randolph into public office." His race pride influenced the Adamses. Randolph was not initially welcomed in political circles because of his race; nevertheless, he persevered. His loyalty to the Democratic Party was rewarded with serving as a delegate to two Democratic National Conventions. He rose in Democratic leadership to serve as "the second chairman of the legislature's black caucus." Lloyd and Victorine would share the same office in the House of Delegates. He filled her position from the Fourth District when she left to serve on City Council.

Marvin Mandel was born in Baltimore on April 19, 1920. He attended local public schools and the University of Maryland. His parents mortgaged their home for him to attend college, making him the first college graduate in his family. He obtained a law degree and entered military service in World War II. After the war, he ran a successful law firm. In 1951, Samuel Friedel suggested he run for the Democratic State Central Committee. In August 2015, the *Baltimore Sun* reported, "[In 1952,] the State Central Committee was faced with the problem of filling a 5th District vacancy in the Baltimore delegation to the House. [Mandel] managed to break a deadlock over a choice for the vacancy by presenting himself as the logical compromise candidate."

His entry into Maryland politics was the beginning of a steady upward climb to the governor's mansion when Spiro T. Agnew left for Washington, D.C., as United States vice president. Marvin served well and ran for two terms. Two months into his second term, he was indicted by a grand jury, along with several associates, for "using his power to push legislation in Annapolis" for personal financial benefit. Convicted on seventeen counts of mail fraud and two counts of racketeering and accepting bribes, he began to serve his term in a federal prison in Florida in 1980. In December 1981, President Ronald Regan commuted his sentence. Marvin's attorneys challenged the conviction, and it was overturned. This reversal allowed the disgraced and disbarred attorney the ability to return to his legal practice.

Mandel died at ninety-five years old. In his memoir, he insisted that he never committed an illegal act as governor. The *Baltimore Sun*'s August 2015 obituary for Mandel notes:

Frank DeFilippo, Mandel's press secretary, said Mandel's hallmark was reforming all three branches of government and creating a system that lives on in Annapolis today. "Marvin Mandel was a transformational governor who bridged the old and the new," he said. "What he did very effectively was take what was a backwater state by the back of the neck and drag it kicking and screaming into what was then the 20th century."

If all politics are local, then Willie had a seat at the table with those elected and innovative persons making deals and inroads in Baltimore. After 1935, his team included Victorine. The intimate details of Willie's businesses did not seemingly concern her, nor did she inquire about them. She respected the line where his business ended and hers as wife began. She lived above reproach in her church attendance, club activities and political aspirations. There were numerous men who worked for and affiliated with Willie. These men acknowledged and at times embraced Victorine. Parks shared strategies and insight with her regarding politics and philanthropy. While other friends would find themselves out for a night at Willie's Club Casino. Marvin Mandel's political career led to the governor's mansion and the Adamses were included. Even when Governor Mandel traveled to Israel to dedicate the Mandel Way, the Adamses were with the Mandel family. Willie's amicable ties and mutual desires brought a bevy of people into Victorine's life. She navigated the host of people through attending dinner parties, hosting events and remaining keenly informed about the quality of life for average Baltimoreans. Mrs. Willie Adams had access to power brokers, influential arenas and unlimited financial resources that served her educational and humanitarian endeavors well into the 1940s and '50s.

The second decade of their marriage would propel Victorine into crusading for a greater political voice for and accountability to African Americans in Baltimore. She understood the link between economic and political power; you needed both to have a lasting and effective impact on the status quo. The remainder of her life was dedicated to civic leadership and community activism to raise awareness of the possibilities available to organized people. African American women, children, urban poor, Catholic minorities and other marginalized people could shift the balance of power when they were informed and organized. The role of Mrs. Willie Adams was a dynamic one suited for Victorine, in part due to her good looks and her rigorous pursuit of equality for all Baltimoreans.

Golfing, Summering at Elktonia Beach and Enjoying Life

Willie and Victorine enjoyed leisure activities. Willie liked golfing, and Victorine preferred the seashore. Their union did not produce children, and their wealth and youth impelled them to socialize in Baltimore's nightlife at Willie's Club Casino, as well as other popular spaces where African Americans could enjoy themselves away from the glare and sting of segregation. Willie's golfing placed him within a solid middle-class culture of professionals who made business deals and strong bonds while walking the course. In 1942, Willie reported from Chicago for the *Afro* the outcome of the Tam O'Shanter National Open and All-American Amateur golf qualifying rounds. There were seven professional golfers, along with several amateurs. One of the pros was Clyde Martin of Chicago, Joe Louis's private pro. Segregation impacted all areas of society, from classrooms to swimming pools to golf courses. In Baltimore, African Americans were restricted to the "colored-only" city-maintained course at Carroll Park.

Heavyweight boxing champion Joe Louis utilized his celebrity status to end discrimination in golfing. After a successful career in boxing from 1937 to 1949, Louis participated in amateur contests around the country, bringing visibility and attention to the inequity in public golf courses. He employed black professionals to tutor him. He also funded his own national tournaments, which at times were interracial in composition. The Joe Louis Open promoted friendly interracial competition and black professional golfers and afforded an alternative sporting leisure option for black people. Louis was an ambassador for the race in sporting after his defeat of Max Schmeling in the boxing ring. The bout had international appeal and signaled a defeat of Adolf Hitler's master race theory. For African Americans, his victory pushed the patriotism and manhood for the race into a global realm that benchmarked the death of ideology of African American inferiority. Even though Louis was unable to destroy public golf course segregation, he did succeed in having the Professional Golfers Association (PGA) remove the "Caucasian-only" clause from its constitution. The PGA, founded in 1916, inserted the discriminatory clause in 1943. Still, African Americans continued to golf and formed their own organization, the United Golfers Association (UGA), in 1926. The UGA created its own Negro National Open tournament from 1926 to 1960. George May, president of the Tam O'Shanter and Country Club, provided African American golfers a space to demonstrate their skill. White professional golfers disregarded the

Willie Adams at
Carroll Park, 1941.
*Victorine Quille Adams
papers, Box 12-14,
folder 27. Courtesy of the
Beulah M. Davis Special
Collections, Morgan State
University.*

Tam O'Shanter tournaments because of their "carnival like atmosphere";
nevertheless, black golfers held tournaments there.

In Baltimore, stringent segregation relegated black golfers to Carroll Park,
which was described by the *Afro* as a "nine-hole affair with sand tees, no
sand traps, no bunkers, no artificial hazards, no flagpoles, no practice green,
one drinking fountain and no basin for washing balls." A city-supported
course, Carroll Park lacked the amenities and investment that white golf
clubs enjoyed, such as a professional course and employees to maintain it.
In July 1942, an all-white superior court jury rendered a verdict "opening
all municipally supported golf courses to colored people." After three days
of testimony on a writ of mandamus filed by D. Arnett Murphy of the *Afro*
against the board of park commissioners, the jury concluded that there was
gross inequity. The park board sought to impede the verdict from becoming
law. George L. Nichols, superintendent of parks, argued that "no golf
professional" applied for usage of Carroll Park's course. Moreover, the park
board argued that the verdict was illegal because Judge Eugene O'Dunne
was not present when the jury returned its verdict. Judge O'Dunne had left
for his summer home in the Blue Ridge Summit. However, in Baltimore
courts, it was customary for the court clerk to receive the verdict. The
park board admitted that the million-dollar budget to maintain the four
municipal courses allotted Carroll Park $21,665, and there were roughly
twelve years of requested improvements that remained unattended. Mount
Pleasant's course was 135 acres, while Carroll Park was 35 acres. The park
board contended that equal treatment did not mean identical treatment.

In December 1942, the Maryland Court of Appeals reversed the
Baltimore City Superior Court's decision. The basis for the reversal "lay
chiefly in an error of the lower court because it denied park commissioners
any discretion." The park commissioners were following state law regarding

Baltimore Colored Golf Course, 1940. *Left to right*: Burns, Carlos, Joe, Willie and Gatey. *Victorine Quille Adams papers, Box 12-14, folder 27. Courtesy of the Beulah M. Davis Special Collections, Morgan State University.*

the separation of the races. Moreover, Judge O'Dunne could order only one course—not all courses—opened to African American golfers. Chief Judge Carroll T. Bond declared that "substantially equal provisions" needed to be made for African American golfers. In May 1943, an agreement was made that provided for immediate improvements at the Carroll Park golf course. The compromise involved Mayor Howard W. Jackson and the city park board allotting $20,000 for alterations and improvements to Carroll Park. Dallas K. Nichols (representing African American golfers) and Preston A. Pairo (representing white golfers) signed an agreement in four terms. Carroll Park would be extended to 3,200 yards from 2,300 yards, and grass greens would replace sand greens. Carroll Park would close until all improvements were made, and then play would resume. During the improvements, "colored golf players shall be admitted without distinction" at the white golf courses. Lastly, once the improvements were done and approved by the chief engineer, Carroll Park would be exclusively for "colored" golfers and the other courses exclusively for white golfers.

It would take seven years for Baltimore to integrate municipally supported golf courses. Judge W. Calvin Chesnut determined that Baltimore violated the Fourteenth Amendment in refusing to allow African American residents "to play on city-owned" golf courses. The improvements to Carroll Park did not provide the remedy to separate but equal. Judge Chesnut declared that "Carroll Park was not substantially equal" to the city courses reserved for whites. The initial complaint filed by D. Arnett Murphy of the *Afro* was enlarged and sponsored by Baltimore's NAACP and the Monumental Golf Association. The mandated improvements to Carroll Park took two years, from 1943 to 1945. The city attorneys applauded their efforts, while Charles Hamilton Houston, Howard Jenkins, Joseph Waddy and W.A.C. Hughes Jr., representing the plaintiff, disagreed. The postwar atmosphere pressed the issues of injustice while men returned home from military service. Moreover, the NAACP crusaded for nearly two decades through local cases that African American citizens were denied due process and protections guaranteed by the Fourteenth Amendment. Various states nullified federal

Baltimore Colored Golf Course. Pugilist Joe Louis is third from the left in white shirt, and Willie is to his right. Sonny Edwards exclusive photograph. *Victorine Quille Adams papers, Box 12-14, folder 27. Courtesy of the Beulah M. Davis Special Collections, Morgan State University.*

laws through "pointing the finger" at private citizens groups that reserved the right to maintain exclusive membership. However, municipalities could not lay claim to such exclusivity because all citizens were entitled rights as citizens and thus entitled to access city-funded services. Willie's passion for golfing and connection to Joe Louis contributed to influencing the decision to desegregate the golf courses. Whether offering testimony or privately funding the cause, Willie's visibility in golfing contributed to improving leisure activities for black Baltimoreans.

Victorine was not a sports enthusiast, but she enjoyed the outdoors. Her favorite haunt, judging by the prolific number of pictures in her collection, was Elktonia Beach. Willie, always looking for new business venues, looked to rural Maryland to purchase a countryside property. African Americans lived along the Eastern Shore and started purchasing property in the 1890s. Frederick Carr, born in the 1840s, purchased 180 acres of land in south Annapolis in 1902. He moved his wife and children to the land and sought to provide a means for betterment for himself and future generations of the Carr family. Farming provided a meager income, so in 1915, Carr opened his property to small groups for picnics and summer boarders. These new endeavors attracted a steady trickle of African Americans seeking clean air and space outside the city. Moreover, the automobile increased the distances African Americans could travel and therefore increased the popularity of Carr's property. Prior to his death in 1928, Carr ensured that the property remain within the Carr family. Two daughters, Florence Sparrow and Elizabeth Smith, bought the remaining shares from siblings who had relocated to other areas. Together, the Carr sisters built up the property, adding overnight cabins that attracted larger groups for longer stays. By 1930, the property had been renamed Carr's View Beach. This prosperous, well-attended seashore space for African Americans attracted Willie Adams. Historian Andrew W. Kahrl notes that "[b]eing able to spend time in quiet rustic retreats, and being there as vacationers and not as laborers, was often cited by leading race men and women as a telltale sign of a rising race."[27] The ability to leave the city in the summer was a clear class indicator of disposable income and the ability to take days from work. Willie, Victorine and other sea-siders were part of the New Negro generation whose "visions of blackness" laid claims to values, success and the "good life," as expressed with upper-class white Americans of that era. They sought to create institutional foundations and spaces where they could breathe and romp free without the glaring reminders of segregation. This concept generated income, elevating the entire African American community "on the pennies

Joe Louis, Louis's trainer Marshall Miles, Willie and an unknown man, circa 1950s. *Victorine Quille Adams papers, Box 12-14, folder 26. Courtesy of the Beulah M. Davis Special Collections, Morgan State University.*

of pleasure seekers" tacitly experiencing proper treatment and economic power, a synergy that would serve the civil rights movement.

In 1944, Willie and business partners formed the Oak Grove Beach Company. Oak Grove purchased acres of waterfront property near Carr's View Beach. Oak Grove opened Elktonia Beach, "an exclusive summer community" for Baltimore's moneyed crowd. In 1948, following the death of Elizabeth Carr, Adams expanded the Oak Grove property and incorporated the original Carr's Beach. Frederick Carr, son of Elizabeth, partnered with Adams to form the Carr's Beach Amusement Company. Adams enriched his holding through partnerships in which he received 51 percent of the profit while allowing the other partner total operational control. Adams was savvy to avoid placing his name on all of his businesses, thus avoiding legal entanglements over taxes and income. By the 1950s, through Adams's connections in New York and Chicago, leading African

Victorine with friends at Elktonia Beach. *Victorine Quille Adams papers, Box 12-14, folder 16. Courtesy of the Beulah M. Davis Special Collections, Morgan State University.*

American entertainers performed at Carr's Beach. All beachgoers and businesses operating at Carr's directly enriched Adams. Kahrl notes that "Adams had a financial stake in virtually every company conducting business on the beach and profited from every aboveboard transaction—from the gate receipts to the slot machines to the concessions."[28]

The activities at Elktonia included beauty contests and youthful activities. There were amusement rides, card games and live concerts. The *Afro* reported, "We all wanted to be independent of a racist white society." Being in a black-owned leisure space surrounded by working-class and wealthy African Americans resulted in admiration for Willie, as well as a symbol of pleasure and pride. Victorine enjoyed the sun, fun and socialization. A natural beauty and self-assured woman, she participated in the beauty contests. She used the opportunity to model accessible refinement to younger women who desired an education and professional career. Located between Baltimore and Washington, D.C., Carr's Beach enjoyed a larger presence due to black radio. Willie formed a partnership with WANN radio station. WANN advertised upcoming entertainers and broadcast live concerts. Charles "Hoppy" Adams "served as the electric master" of Carr's entertainment events.[29] The *Afro*'s Rambling Rose wrote, "Hoppy Adams was a philanthropist and gave money anonymously to those who needed it. He helped musicians get a start by playing their first recording on the air."

For Victorine, the seaside visits garnered more than relaxation; they provided her with beneficial contacts. African American entertainers endured segregation in ugly and unique ways throughout America. Their music was popular in most markets, yet they were denied equitable treatment. Places like Carr's were enjoyable reprieves. Performers could enjoy the sun, sand and privacy offered by Sparrow's Beach. At times, several entertainers would be coming and going, so fellowship refreshed their spirits. The integration of public beaches signaled the death knell of the Carr's Beach Amusement Company. The modernization of highways and bridge construction opened more areas along the Eastern Shore for summering options. The land was sold for residential development. However, the New Negro held a larger vision for the race. Their fight was not only in the cities for the right to live where they could afford. They also demanded equality in the distribution of municipal funding for schools, golf courses and social services. While basking in the seashore's sun listening to their entertainers, the New Negro expanded the concept of "economic self-determination" through owning rustic spaces. In these spaces, they collectively breathed non-segregated air and celebrated their financial heroes who acquired property and offered top-notch leisurely recreation.

Left to right: Mr. Charles Win, proprietor of Elktonia Beach; Victorine; and Willie. *Victorine Quille Adams papers, Box 12-14, folder 16. Courtesy of the Beulah M. Davis Special Collections, Morgan State University.*

Victorine (*second from the right, front row*) seated beside Claudia Black, Willie's mother, at Elktonia Beach. *Victorine Quille Adams papers, Box 12-14, folder 16. Courtesy of the Beulah M. Davis Special Collections, Morgan State University.*

Their personal proclivities—his golfing and hers seaside romping—held more than leisurely pursuits. They are examples of how the Adamses were united in their vision for a better life for African Americans in general and black Baltimoreans in particular. Their race pride impelled them to assist those striving, model for young people and provide support to existing businesses throughout the community. Economic power strengthened the community; however, political power would ensure that lawmakers included black people and their interests when crafting legislation. The future was bright for the wealthy and well-connected couple. Willie's vast array of business interests and political contacts positioned him as a powerbroker in Baltimore. Victorine grew in social stature from his success. World War II offered African Americans yet another chance to display their patriotism and valor in military service. In 1935, Mary McLeod Bethune founded the National Council of Negro Women in Washington, D.C. The NCNW would serve as a lobbying agency on behalf of hundreds of Negro women's organizations. The collective voice of Negro women and children needed to crescendo into a measured and deliberate fashion, from the farms to the university classrooms to the housewives and domestic workers. Willie worked his calling through business. The 1940s would witness Victorine finding her calling among women in the spirit of Bethune. Organizing women and harnessing the power of their voice and numbers in Baltimore existed in small episodes; however, that energy needed to be harnessed and targeted on a particular topic without wavering.

Victorine and Willie were secure in their relationship and comfortably ensconced in the community. They moved from McCullough Street to Carlisle Avenue in the all-white Hanlon Park neighborhood in the summer of 1949. In 1948, he purchased a retail space and opened the Charm Center, the "only black owned and operated" clothing store for women in Baltimore. Segregation prevented African Americans from shopping in major department stores; if they gained access, it was implied that they were picking up packages for their employers. Many black women traveled to Philadelphia or New York to purchase couture. Victorine managed the Charm Center. She held fashion shows, private viewings and political organization meetings there. The Charm Center was located at 1811 Pennsylvania Avenue, the main thoroughfare on the west side. Even though Victorine ended her classroom teaching career in 1945, she continued to educate through fashion shows and lectures on politics. In October 1960, she held a fashion show styled "just for school Marms" attending a state teachers' conference in Baltimore.

Concurrently, her ties to schoolteachers ran through her sorority connections, political activism and the Charm Center. She innovated Project Beauty and Charm, a six-week course offered to female Model City residents ages eighteen and up. Project Beauty instilled in students the know-how to improve their poise, charm and appearance. Upon graduation, one of the ladies from the group was chosen as the most improved through "enhance[ing] her beauty" and garnered a special award. All participants were required to attend four of the five sessions offered in order to receive a certificate. The courses were instructed by beauty consultant coordinators. The training and technical assistance program site was an office at 2510 St. Paul Street. The five sessions included: Body Beautiful, taught by Victorine; Makeup and Skin, taught by Miss J.P. Scott; Hair Grooming, taught by Mrs. Rose G. Byrd; Manners and Charm, taught by Mrs. Clarice Brooks; and Fashion and Posture, taught by Mrs. Pinnie Ross and Mrs. Rosalind Hanks. A fashion show accompanied the graduation service. In 1954, the Charm

Left to right: Willie and Victorine, Mr. and Mrs. Clyde Martin, Mr. and Mrs. Walter and Ruby Thomas, Kleco Club on Pressman Street. *Victorine Quille Adams papers, Box 12-14, folder 20. Courtesy of the Beulah M. Davis Special Collections, Morgan State University.*

Center held a net value of $80,000, which is equivalent to roughly $733,000 in 2018 dollar value. Through the Charm Center, Victorine engaged all strata of black women. She hired attractive workers who serviced customers and modeled fashions on stage and for high-end customers.

In February 1955, the Charm Center provided styles for a fashion show sponsored by Phi Delta Kappa, Gamma Chapter. The benefit fashion show sought to raise funds for the Children's Division of Crownsville State Hospital. The General Assembly of Maryland opened the Hospital for the Negro Insane in 1910. The state purchased a 556-acre farm as a model of self-sufficiency to treat mentally ill black residents. By 1912, the hospital had become Crownsville. The patients were exploited and built structures, milked cows and planted and harvested crops. The facility was often overcrowded and underfunded. Zosha Stuckey purports that the intolerant racial climate in Baltimore directly impacted the increase in residents at Crownsville. Stuckey's research indicates that many African Americans were sent to Crownsville for innocuous reasons such as alcoholism. The real reason for people being placed at Crownsville was racial hygiene

Willie and Victorine in Greece. *Victorine Quille Adams papers, Box 12-14, folder 23. Courtesy of the Beulah M. Davis Special Collections, Morgan State University.*

Willie and Victorine as guests of President Lyndon B. Johnson at White House. *Victorine Quille Adams papers, Box 12-14, folder 20. Courtesy of the Beulah M. Davis Special Collections, Morgan State University.*

cleansing the city streets of the "Negro invasion." Paul Lurz, who worked at Crownsville, salvaged records from the hospital at its closing in 2004. Throughout its existence, patients were mistreated and subject to medical experimentation. Current scholarship informs us that abusive behavior was not unusual for mental health facilities; however, the racially motivated factor at Crownsville attracted the attention of black Baltimore residents and the NAACP, seeking to humanize the treatment of intellectually challenged citizens. Unfortunately, Crownsville did not live long enough to redeem its reputation. The attention and funds raised by Phi Delta Kappa sought to ameliorate the conditions patients endured while at Crownsville. By 1955, Maryland was moving toward desegregation of all mental institutions.

Victorine and Willie maintained a healthy work-life balance. They traveled, vacationed, participated in leisure activities and invested in their community. They did not allow racism, segregation or other discriminatory practices in Baltimore to diminish their personal worth or the value of their people. They opted to live their best lives and determined that they would provide a solution to problems caused by racism, ignorance and silence. Together, with friends and through organized endeavors, Victorine and Willie carved out a space for themselves while providing opportunities for others. Victorine's foray into politics ran parallel to the government investigation into illegal gambling and some of Willie's businesses. Together, they weathered the several trials, numerous investigations and an allegedly incriminating wiretap. Victorine was not swayed by testimony or evidence. They both remained committed to each other and racial uplift through humanitarian methods.

Chapter 3

RESPECTABILITY POLITICS AND SPEAKING TRUTH

Empowered

The idea of respectability was the principal basis where African Americans asserted their right to equality as American citizens. This concept—expressed through dress, articulation of speech, socialization and aspirations—remained a fixture within the black community from Reconstruction to the modern civil rights movement. In brief, it said we are worthy of fair treatment because we demonstrate and model exemplary behavior. For Victorine, her life was circumscribed by this understanding, and she could not live beneath that expectation. Her dress, deportment, speech and appearance were measured within the black community and throughout the white world. She walked a fine line between the two worlds as an accountable and informed ambassador. Stephanie Shaw, in *What a Woman Ought to Be and Do*, chronicled three generations of professional African American women born from 1880 to 1950. Shaw concludes that "these women did not stumble upon these leadership roles accidentally; nor were they, in general born to them....They achieved leadership through an empowering socialization process and a particular understanding of womanhood—and how they experienced it." Victorine's experience in home, church, college, classroom and marriage impressed upon her a sense of stewardship. To accomplish this aim, she connected with organizations and individuals that held similar values and desired similar outcomes. Throughout her life, black women teachers and social workers crusaded for equality on behalf of the community.

MAKING THE WORLD A BETTER PLACE: NATIONAL COUNCIL OF NEGRO WOMEN

On December 5, 1935, in New York, Mary McLeod Bethune called together the leaders of nearly ten organizations. They voted to become a permanent organization, named the National Council of Negro Women. "Born in the dreary and tumultuous mid-thirties, its struggle for existence paralleled the struggle which the nation was passing through. The world, [in a] frightening and continuous global crises that finally impaled the entire world in war, caught the Council up in the vortex. The purpose of the [NCNW] was definitely chartered by the gravity of the time."[30]

Some in attendance questioned the intentions of another organization and potential disunity. Yet on April 29, 1936, in Sojourner Truth Hall at Howard University, the fledgling group adopted its constitution and elected permanent officers. Among the slate of candidates were president, Mary McLeod Bethune; first vice president, Dr. Charlotte Hawkins Brown; fourth vice president, Mary Church Terrell; and executive secretary, Dean Lucy D. Slowe, a Baltimore native. On July 25, 1936, they were incorporated with the principal business address of Dean Lucy Slowe's campus office. Lucy Diggs Slowe was the first female scholarship winner and graduate from the Baltimore Colored School to enter Howard University. During her matriculation, she co-founded Alpha Kappa Alpha Sorority, Incorporated. She continued her education at Columbia University and became the first dean of women at Howard University. Her career in education migrated through the classroom to administration to writing policy. She sought to optimize the potential of Negro women through education, exposure and organization, creating the Association of Deans of Women and Advisers to Girls in Negro Schools. The association provided viable connections and communication between all the HBCU campuses where deans and advisers worked with students and other women's groups.

The NCNW certificate of incorporation adopted four purposes for its organization: to unite national member organizations in a NCNW; to educate, encourage and effect the participation of Negro women in civic, political, economic and educational activities and institutions; to serve as a clearing house for the dissemination of activities concerning women; and to plan, initiate and carry out projects that develop, benefit and integrate the Negro and the nation.

During its infancy, programing advocated for black women while collecting, publishing and disseminating facts about Negro women's life in

America. To combat segregation, they offered job training and counseling to provide women with the skills needed to secure employment. The workshops focused on skills, dress, conversation and patriotism, precluding any obvious reason for denying a well-trained woman a job. The war effort provided an international stage for Negro women to show themselves able. Lastly, NCNW utilized the black press to foster better race relations. Bethune was a master spokeswoman and believed her deportment, speech and knowledge proved a living example of Negro women's potential. NCNW published a journal and newsletter for its membership and planned for archives to document its accomplishments. Bethune's scheduled hair appointments, facials and fine clothing warred with her desire to remain totally connected to her humble beginnings. As a global ambassador for Negro women whose history was mired in derogatory stereotypes in print, films and literature, her example and NCNW would be viable counterpoints and testimonies to an ugly history. This powerful sense of purpose attracted Victorine and aligned with her self-perception.

On December 18, 1943, NCNW leadership and legal committee consented to the purchase of the property at 1318 Vermont Avenue, Washington, D.C. This property was located three blocks from the White House and squarely within a rising black community. Bethune sought individual assistance in upgrading the property and furnishing the rooms. The renovations and outfitting of the property took nearly a year. Once everything was in place, NCNW dedicated the building on October 15, 1944.

The program was held in front of the property. Charlotte Hawkins Brown offered comments, stating:

> [The NCNW headquarters] *stands for unity of purpose and ideals; it is an open sesame to united endeavors to prove to the world that Negro womanhood can go forward to battle against the evils and handicaps that beset the paths of all women notwithstanding their struggle for the enjoyment of rights and privileges vouchsafed to the womanhood of all other races and denied to them....Let* [it] *not be said that we dedicate this building to Negro womanhood alone, for if democracy is to be a reality in our beloved America, white women, black women, red women, yellow women must find their way through these doors and in consultation, meditation and prayer approach world problems under the guidance of Almighty God.*[31]

In 1943, Baltimore women opened their chapter of NCNW. The five charter members were Kate Sheppard, Juanita Mitchell, Vivian Alleyne,

Emma Dudley and Victorine Adams. Three women were teachers, one a lawyer and the other a political organizer. Formally, the Metropolitan Council of Baltimore sought to address social needs and political changes in the city. In 1970, the name changed to Greater Baltimore Section–NCNW. Kate Sheppard, a personal friend of Bethune, is credited with being instrumental in bringing NCNW to Baltimore. Vivian Alleyne was elected president in 1947 but was unable to remain in office due to a personal matter. Vivian came to Baltimore in 1930 as a secretary for the YWCA. A college graduate, she taught kindergarteners. Involved in collegiate organizations and well-traveled, she continued advocating for equality. She became president of the League of Women's Clubs and served as executive secretary for the Non Partisan Voters League. Juanita Mitchell served as the program committee chair. Her programming brought notable women to Baltimore. Juanita graduated from Douglass High School in 1927. She felt the sting of racism when she was denied admission to Johns Hopkins University. A graduate of University of Maryland's law school, she committed her life to eliminating segregation in municipal and state facilities. Her impact was doubled through her husband's involvement with the NAACP. Emma Dudley belonged to the Maryland League of Women's Clubs. Victorine served as secretary until 1948. During her early years with NCNW, she experienced great gain and loss. In 1945, her mother, Estelle Tate, passed away. This did not stop her participation, but I believe it curtailed her frequency of participation. In 1946, she founded the Colored Women's Democratic Campaign Committee, and in 1948, she opened the Charm Center. Willie purchased the retail space, and Victorine operated the day-to-day activities. Morphing from teacher to business and club woman, Victorine acquired a certificate from the New York School of Retailing in June 1954 to implement best practices in selling women's clothing. These two endeavors provided the foundational support she needed to expand her vision of increased political and economic empowerment for black Baltimoreans. The activities and connections she made in the NCNW served her well, providing insight and inroads to the connectedness of the needs facing urban dwellers.

In 1945, Mattie Coasey was elected president of the Baltimore chapter of the NCNW. Coasey moved to Baltimore in 1920. As the daughter of an AME bishop and wife of a medical doctor, meeting the needs of less fortunate people was an innate and socialized characteristic of her life. Upon arrival, she involved herself in YWCA and Eastern Stars. She drove for the Red Cross and became known throughout Baltimore for helping young people. She appreciated a touch of human kindness in all relationships. Her

Metropolitan Council of Baltimore, National Council of Negro Women. *Victorine Quille Adams papers, Box 12-14, folder 19. Courtesy of the Beulah M. Davis Special Collections, Morgan State University.*

administration established the presence of the NCNW in Baltimore as one of humanity, vigilance, activism and cooperation. During her administration, the Baltimore NCNW galvanized sorority women and national leadership from NCNW to send delegates to a hearing on Maryland's Jim Crow repeal bill. The membership of the Metropolitan Council was an extensive network that spanned the diverse interests of the membership. In 1946, its affiliate representation from established groups were ten organizations that served as delegates. Beauticians, church women, collegiate sororities and professional guilds were listed. The chapter had sixteen subcommittees. Employment, family life, consumer education, rural life, youth, historian, reporter, postwar planning and programming were listed and occupied by women such as Lillie Jackson, Verda Welcome, Mary E. Hawkins and Juanita Mitchell. These women, along with the executive council, were well connected, and their additional connects benefited the larger community and enriched local programming.

On April 5, 1945, Victorine wrote to Bethune on behalf of the Metropolitan Council. At issue was an investigation NCNW sought to pursue regarding Truman Gibson and the all–African American 92nd Division.

Formed in World War I, the 92nd Division had white officers. Gibson's report implied that black servicemen were "not good fighting material." Victorine informed Bethune that women had letters from servicemen who indicated that Gibson often accepted the report of white officers without inquiring from the servicemen on the behavior in question. In 1945, General Edward M. Almond commanded the 92nd and "faulted" their race as the reason for seemingly failed attacks on German troops. Victorine noted, "As wives, mothers, sweethearts of many Baltimore men with the 92nd Division, we protest this unwarranted attack [and question the source] of the report."[32]

Gibson's report was cited by virulent racists on the "unfitness" of black servicemen. In October 1946, Gibson attacked the military's "Army Bias" toward African Americans. Finis Austin, of the *Afro*, linked Gibson's new-found voice to a repentance moment of new-found conscience. The postwar tirade on the unfairness within the military did not benefit the 500,000 soldiers or the men of the 92nd Division. Finis wrote, "It will take more than a post-war verbal attack upon the Army by [him] to cause them to forgive or forget a deal which, in their opinion, has had no equal since the days of Judas Iscariot." In the same letter, Victorine mentioned the unfair treatment WACs were having at Fort Devans; however, Bethune and the NCNW were already investigating allegations. Victorine wrote, "[Already] on the job before I could get the letter written. Congratulations!! I read the splendid report. Thank God you were in there and on time!! More power to you and your splendid workers."[33]

The 1946 Metropolitan Council Annual Report highlighted activities sponsored throughout the year. In March, a meeting at Sharp Street Methodist Church presented Helen Gahagan Douglas and Dr. Vivian Carter Mason. Douglas was a starlet turned politician. She served as a congresswoman who met Bethune through Eleanor Roosevelt. In Congress, she focused on housing shortages and racial equality. Mason was the third president of the NCNW. Elected in 1953, she worked closely with Bethune. Her four-year administration introduced a more sophisticated administration and enlarged programming agenda. The rising civil rights struggle occupied her administration. After her presidency, Mason urged women to get involved in politics. Through political education, women have the right to share in the legislative process, as well as broaden the concept of fair governance. The annual report mentioned the presentation of Vera Scott, who spoke on juvenile delinquency. The informative presentation empowered the members to innovate ways to lessen delinquency. In May, Sarah Fernandis, first vice president of the Civic League of Baltimore, spoke on "pioneering Negro women" in Maryland, emboldening the members to know the strength of their foremothers.

In 1948, Bethune came to Baltimore in her nationwide endeavor to increase the membership of NCNW. The membership enlistment efforts desired to fill the NCNW rolls with 500,000 women of all races. The campaign theme, United for Human and Civil Rights, embraced President Harry S. Truman's platform to implement civil rights legislation and interaction throughout America. Human and civil rights benefited not only people of color but also women who were denied access to certain jobs and opportunities. Bethune invited all to a benefit concert at Carnegie Hall, where Carol Brice, a nationally known singer, performed. The concert was well attended but did not generate the revenue or surge in membership desired. The Metropolitan Council raised money to support the work of the national organization.

The constellation of women that composed the Metropolitan Council, as well as those who presented lectures, contributed to the growing vision of civic activism within Victorine. These women were wives, sorority members, church workers, professionals and politically conscious citizens whose numbers nudged a space at the table. These women brought ideas of equality, fairness and humanity for all citizens regardless of race, color or creed. Many were peers of Victorine and therefore familiar with the sting of segregation and the crippling effects it had on rising generations of young people. The inequity within Baltimore city reached the steps of the statehouse in Annapolis. The black press reported indignities, the NAACP filed suit in court and the Urban League maintained an unrelenting account of statistical research on progress within cities around the county. Through the NCNW's national network and coordinated efforts, the days of Jim Crow, black women's invisibility and the silence of poor urban minority populations were numbered.

COLORED WOMEN'S DEMOCRATIC CAMPAIGN COMMITTEE: ROCKING THE VOTE

In 1946, Victorine organized the Colored Women's Democratic Campaign Committee (CWDCC), whose motto was, "If democracy is worth fighting for, it's worth voting for." Its members sought to welcome all women; register all and enlighten all; interest more women in politics; stimulate and educate the public on the value of the ballot; register more voters; get

Colored Women's Democratic Campaign Committee voter education session. Victorine is at the front right. The candidate being discussed is Philip H. Goodman (1914–1976). Goodman was a member of the Maryland Senate from Baltimore City District 5 (1955–60). He was then elected president of the Baltimore City Council and became mayor of Baltimore on December 6, 1962. Clinton's Studio. *Victorine Quille Adams papers, Box 12-15, folder 5. Courtesy of the Beulah M. Davis Special Collections, Morgan State University.*

out the vote at election time; and take part in the civic, political and social progress of the city.

The CWDCC affiliated with the Red Cross, NAACP Community Fund, Urban League, League of Women's Clubs, Association to Abolish the Poll Tax, Women's League for Peace and Freedom–Send a Girl to Camp. Its regular activities included meeting on the first Tuesday of each month. Within its first years, members visited the White House and United Nations and worked for the election of Governor William Preston Lane Jr. with a cash contribution to his campaign fund. They worked to mobilize support for Mayor Theodore R. McKeldin, other white politicians and African American politicians sympathetic to their community issues. They launched a voter registration drive and canvassed homes and friends to get potential voters. On the street, they used cars donated by interested people to spread the idea of voting in local elections. They used PTA meetings, churches, schools, phone calls and all other social connections to promote the necessity and benefits of voting. The visits to the White House and United Nations resulted in partnering with the NCNW. The interconnectedness of the CWDCC, NCNW and Victorine enlarged her impact. The synergy of Bethune's global presence and husband Willie's city and state contacts positioned Victorine at the front of a loosely configured pool of black women voters. Her vision to confederate the women across political parties, economic and marital status, religious affiliation, employment and complexion crossed barriers that impeded the success potential of black women voters.

Their future plans included visits to City Council, the mayor's office and the governor's mansion. The CWDCC hosted benefit parties for charity and to help with registration drives, increase membership and organize the districts, ward by ward, precinct by precinct and block by block. Members ultimately desired to establish a permanent registration council on a nonpartisan basis, to elect more African Americans, help

Red Cross team. Victorine is at the center; to her left is Willard Allen, most worshipful grand master, Prince Hall Masons of Maryland, and second from the right on the front row is Dr. Lillie C. Jackson, president of the Baltimore Branch of the NAACP. *Victorine Quille Adams papers, Box 12-14, folder 10. Courtesy of the Beulah M. Davis Special Collections, Morgan State University.*

abolish the Jim Crow laws and run a woman for public office to be better Americans in a better America. Victorine kept the membership informed and engaged through a system of delegates who were assigned to attend public meetings, gather information and report back to the body. In March 1949, Lillian Hebron was assigned to the park board and City Council, and Ruth Turner was assigned to the school board and city planning meetings. If questioned about their presence and their organizational affiliation, the women were to state: "Just here for a visit to see how the board works." They were representatives of the CWDCC or affiliate, and there might be other members seeking to attend board meetings. Victorine implored the women to be mindful of their appearance:

> *Do not overdress, be neat, wear a hat and gloves no slips showing, please no loud talking. Be alert at all times, speak clearly, if called upon, give your name and title.* [Make sure to] *mention Miss or Mrs. Registered voter and interested in good government. Take a friend with you if you can, the more the merrier. However, only the delegate or alternate will be paid. If you cannot go at the appointed time—let us know or better still get a substitute—*[a lady] *in the club.*[34]

Members were reimbursed for bus fare and lunch. Delegates were encouraged to keep most of their observations in their minds. Victorine desired to have the delegates write little to keep the boards open to the free flow of information at their meetings. Through these tactics, delegates reported back on a wealth of issues. In one park board meeting in June 1949, Hebron reported about a contest over Clifton Park. The discussion became heated when "colored children" were being considered to use the space for recreation. A delegation of more than fifty whites attended the meeting and asked the board to reverse its decision allowing the East Baltimore children use of the proposed recreation facilities. They wanted the neighborhood to remain white. Hebron reported that the mayor was key, since board appointments were done by him. Toward this end, the decisions would improve once the board was occupied by fair-minded people.

They contributed to the successful campaign and election of Harry A. Cole to the State Senate. Cole was born into a working-class family in Washington, D.C., in 1921. When his father died, his mother moved the family to Baltimore, her hometown. The Cole family adapted to life in Baltimore. Cole attended the segregated public schools and obtained his undergraduate degree from Morgan State in 1943. He served in the army

Democratic Women visit congressmen in D.C. *Left to right*: Victorine, Congressman George Fallon, Congressman Edward Garmatz, Gloria Cole, Congressman Samuel N. Friedel and Gladys Barbour. *Victorine Quille Adams papers, Box 12-15, folder 6. Courtesy of the Beulah M. Davis Special Collections, Morgan State University.*

in World War II, participating in combat in Europe and the Pacific theater. He obtained a law degree in 1949 from the University of Maryland. Soon after graduation, he was the first black lawyer hired as an assistant state attorney general to provide legal advice. His campaign for the State Senate as a Republican seemed impossible. James H. "Jack" Pollack, a "political broker," exercised "nearly absolute control" in areas on the west side. According to historian Matthew Crenson, since the 1920s, the Democratic Party in Baltimore had "limited leverage" with black voters. Crenson notes that "[p]atronage and favors attracted a minority of Black Baltimoreans to the Democrats."[35] Principally, African Americans were Republicans, the party of Abraham Lincoln. The Democratic Party was the one with a "Confederate heritage" and obtuse racial ideas that muted the needs of African Americans. The election of Franklin D. Roosevelt ushered in a new era of Democrats who seemingly sought to provide for the underdog and marginalized people, both black and white. Concurrently, the formation

Honorable Harry A. Cole, November 1954. *Victorine Quille Adams papers, Box 12-14, folder 2. Courtesy of the Beulah M. Davis Special Collections, Morgan State University.*

of the Black Cabinet, in which Bethune participated, further endeared Roosevelt Democrats to the black community.

In Baltimore, segregation and overt racism threatened the expanding Democratic Party. Crenson notes that "as African American voters transferred their loyalties to the Democratic Party in the 1930s, the avoidance of racial politics became not just a matter of preserving domestic tranquility but an essential condition for preserving the city's majority party."[36] Similar to the nation, the white-black balance needed to be maintained unless southern whites were antagonized and leave the party. The tenuous threads benefited Pollack, whose political territory included judges and city and state lawmakers. Toward this end, Crenson notes, black-white alliances could form because race was a bargaining chip where black votes enriched white politicians. When Cole announced his bid for State Senate, this disturbed Pollack's plans and selected candidate. In 1954, Cole defeated a Pollack candidate. Cole's success initiated the unraveling of Pollack's vice-like grip on the west side. Cole's victory was not without contention. The November results were being rechecked by December because of the slim margin of thirty-seven votes and one voter's signature. Bernard Melnicove lost to Cole and sought to have the ballots checked. Melnicove's needling, according to the *Afro*, sought to wrest the election win from Cole. The *Afro* reported that Cole spent $2,279.50 on the campaign, while Melnicove spent $618.97. On October 16, a dinner was hosted to benefit the coalition ticket for incumbent Theodore McKeldin for governor, as well as support for Cole. Held at Sharp Street Church, the dais was ecumenical, as well as representative of black Baltimore's elite. Dwight Holmes of Morgan, Linwood G. Koger of Monumental Bar Association, Henry G. Parks of Parks Sausages, Robert B. Watts of the NAACP and Victorine of the CWDCC shared greetings. The meal was catered by Park Sausages. The contributors to Cole's campaign donated $1,338; among the donors were fraternity brothers and Morgan State employees. Ultimately, the recheck found no fraud in the election, and Cole was sworn in as the first African American state senator in Maryland.

This victory proved that an informed and organized voting community could effect change.

Cole introduced a piece of civil rights legislation. In March 1955, he introduced Senate Bill #219. The civil rights bill sought to provide equal rights for all persons in certain places of public accommodation, resort or amusement. The bill sought to ensure that all persons within Maryland would be entitled to full and equal accommodation, advantages and facilities. Moreover, exclusion on race, creed, national origin or ancestry would be unlawful. Businesses and publicly owned places would be fined $100 to $500 if violating this proposed law. In April 1955, the penalty clause killed the civil rights bill. The "criminal penalties" resulted in white Republicans abandoning Cole and aligning with the Democrats. One Republican senator noted that progress takes time, and therefore, penalizing people for attempting to change is unfair. Another senator believed that rather than force legislation, education and cooperation should be attempted. Cole only served one term in the State Senate; he lost in 1958 to a Pollack-backed candidate. His inaugural victory cracked open the potential for black voters. In his 1999 obituary, Victorine stated, "[He] opened the floodgates because his victory proved we could do it."

Victorine viewed the work of the CWDCC as more than an agent of political education but a calling to serve the race and social justice. There was an induction ceremony similar to collegiate sororities. A candlelight service for the organization of wards incorporated biblical scripture and elements of character. The ritual afforded future participants an opportunity to understand the aims of the CWDCC and agree to those terms as viable members. The ritual included a leader and several candle-bearers and messengers. The leader stated: "To every-thing there is a season, and a time to every-thing under the heaven. A time to be born, and a time to die; a time to plant, and a time to pluck up that which is planted; a time to kill, and a time to heal; a time to break down and a time to build up." (Ecclesiastes 3:1–4)[37]

The leader continued to state:

> *This then, is our time to build up our organization and there-by help build up democracy in our time. Except the Lord build the house, they labor in vain that build it, Psalms 12. May He in His almighty wisdom help us build wisely and with strength and conviction the C.W.D.C.C. is like a house that needs to be built on a larger scale. So, we the members of that body have seen fit to welcome a new addition to our house the women of the 16th ward.*[38]

The initiates were called to "exemplify all the aims and ambitions of the Mother Group," which was the CWDCC. Once they consented, a series of colored candles was lit to express the aims of the CWDCC. First was the red candle, which symbolized the Mother Group/Parent Body of all "colored women democrats" in Maryland. It symbolized all their aims, ambitions and secret hopes. The ritual states that "[f]rom the Parent Body other candles will be lighted, the lights from which will lead all women along the paths of social progress, civic advancement and political power. These evidences of progress shall be realized by our aims. It is fitting and proper that the first candle be lighted from the Parent Body is held by Mrs. Ruth White, a charter member of the CWDCC and a resident of the 16th ward."[39]

In the notes, the CWDCC implored initiates to embrace the larger needs of black women, which was sympathetic to the main aim of the CWDCC. The CWDCC was interested in more than women in politics. The red candle

Democratic Women entertain the Balto Bullets, honoring them for their integration policies. *Left to right, women only*: Ruth Turner, Zelma Johnson, Ada Smith, Victorine, Tim Hawkins and M.C. Pictured also is Dr. Barksdale. *Victorine Quille Adams papers, Box 12-15, folder 3. Courtesy of the Beulah M. Davis Special Collections, Morgan State University.*

lighter stated, "Too long has the Negro woman neglected this important phase of potential, thus, the members of this organization pledge themselves to do every-thing possible to interest more of our women in politics."[40]

Mrs. Alma Foster, a charter member of the CWDCC and resident of the Sixteenth Ward, voiced another aim to register more voters. Foster charged, "Many of the people in the 16th ward are new there. Some are not registered. We must register them. Some need to change their address. We must work on that too. There is much to be done in this section. We must register more voters."[41]

Mrs. Verda Welcome, a resident of the Sixteenth Ward and member of CWDCC, stated, "As women of a political group we must aim to stimulate and educate the public on the value of the ballot. All of the ills that confront us could be eliminated or greatly relieved by the skillful use of the ballot at election time. We must teach our people to vote not for men—but for issues."[42] Mrs. Clotelia Coleman, a member of the CWDCC and resident of the Sixteenth Ward, remarked, "We women Democrats aim to get out the vote at election time. All of our labors will be in vain if the registered

Skating party for junior registration cups, sponsored by Democratic Women and Parks Sausages Company. All children were encouraged to ring doorbells and get out the vote. Chuck Richards awarded prizes for the talent contest. Free refreshments and free admission were offered to all the parties. Victorine is in the front with striped bag; Henry Parks is the tall man in the second row. *Victorine Quille Adams papers, Box 12-11, folder 26. Courtesy of the Beulah M. Davis Special Collections, Morgan State University.*

people won't vote on Election Day, so, we aim to get out the vote."[43] Mrs. Nikki Randolph, a member of the CWDCC, celebrated her husband as an inspiration for the CWDCC. She credited his foresight and vision as a factor in forming the CWDCC. "We democratic women want to take an active part in the civic and social activities of the community as well as the political ones. Each is dependent on the other. So, we must meet our social obligations and partake of the civic responsibilities, too."[44]

There are eight subsets of women's division in the Sixteenth Ward. Mrs. Vivian Alleyne was the female leader of the district, and Dr. R.L. Jackson was the male leader. It would be Alleyne's responsibility to help organize the other wards in her district. Some of the women in her district were Mrs. Beatrice Pitts, Mrs. Phyllis Walston, Miss Valeris Butler, Mrs. Clarence Williams, Mrs. Edith Bailey and Mrs. Mary Johns. The initiates were reminded that "to realize CWDCC aims," certain attributes were needed to build strength of character. They had to promise to build characters and strength of character on behalf of the organization. The subsequent candles symbolized trust, hope, humility, unity, courage, truth and charity. The CWDCC expounded on these traits:

Trust—We must have trust in our organization, in ourselves and in each other. Without trust we cannot succeed. All respond: we promise to keep the trust placed in us.

Hope—We must have hope in ourselves, each other and our organization. Without hope there would be no salvation. Let us pray for hope. We promise to have hope.

Humility—May our hearts be not haughty nor our eyes lofty. Without humility with our lesser endowed—we cannot achieve our goal. We promise to have humility.

Unity—How good and pleasant it is for brethren to dwell together in unity. Unity is a precious ointment. In unity there is strength. We must unite to win. We promise to keep unified.

Courage—Courage to see the light, courage to find the way, courage to face the issue, courage to go on after a crushing defeat, courage to stand alone. These trials are the test of courage. We promise to have courage.

Truth—Knowledge and love. There is no truth without knowledge—no love without truth. Grant that we have an abundance of truth, knowledge and love. We promise truth, knowledge and love.

Charity—Charity is the [essence] of unity, truth and hope. Without charity we are nothing. We promise to have charity.[45]

Toward the end, the leader intoned, "The lights are all glowing—darkness has receded—the shadows of doubt and fear disappear with the advent of the flames. These flames signify all we stand for—a house of many mansions built on charity, truth, knowledge, love, courage, unity, humility, hope, trust, and of course our basic aims."[46] In closing, Victorine expressed deep appreciation for the women of the Sixteenth Ward. She noted "the courage they have exhibited in being the first ward to be organized in our democratic set-up the first mansion in our house. May we be blessed, may heaven smile upon us, may we be worthy of the trust. Welcome the women of the 16th ward."[47]

The organization made the political process relatable through teaching about the issues, learning about the candidates and realizing there was power in unity. The CWDCC also incorporated additional aspects of political consciousness and empowerment. Through subtle and direct intention, its members sought to interest more women in politics; stimulate and educate the public on the value of the ballot; register more voters; get voters out to the polls at election time; and take an active part in the social and civic, as well as the political, activities of the community. Incremental, ongoing involvement in political education and voting would shift the attention of politicians and future politicians to the African American community. These women would command the respect as a voting bloc that could sway local and state elections in favor of particular candidates whose platform included civil rights matters. The success with Harry Cole afforded the women a glimpse into understanding the process and realizing the need to position themselves accordingly. In 1996, on the occasion of its fiftieth anniversary, the CWDCC celebrated its accomplishment in raising political awareness, identifying qualified candidates and registering thousands to vote. It thanked the men who contributed to its success: Askew Gatewood, attorney; Carl Murphy, *Afro American* newspaper publisher; Willie Adams, businessman; and Clarence "Du" Burns, politician. There were men who served as a transportation and publicity brigade in the early years of the CWDCC. Through dedicated effort, the election of two African American women became a reality with the election of Verda Welcome to the State Senate and Victorine to the Baltimore City Council.

Sisters Indeed: Sorority Life in Baltimore

Victorine's career in teaching afforded her an opportunity to see the intimate connectedness of women. In 1900, women composed 75 percent of the public school teachers. Those numbers would continue to grow upward of 80 percent while men entered teaching with aspirations for administrative positions. A feature of black college life since 1908 with the founding of Alpha Kappa Alpha Sorority at Howard University was sorority life. In the early years, the sororities provided networking and cultural enrichment for college-educated women. Their race, gender and educational attainment placed them far from the average American women and galaxies apart from the majority of African American women. This unique position afforded these women the opportunity to become advocates and agents of change on behalf of the race, themselves and future generations. The field of education was a logical place for women to organize to the benefit of their salaries, their students and the race. In Baltimore, the public school teachers of Victorine's era were segregated and placed in municipally operated and consistently underfunded schools. These injustices were met with protest. Their early protests demanded pay equity and adequate supplies. In the 1940s, teachers joined organizations such as NCNW and the CWDCC to advocate for social justice issues. Also, by the 1940s, numerous Greek-lettered organizations formed around professions and spread across the country, linking through college campuses, churches and the black press. Many published their own journals informing, sharing and planning strategies to usher in change. In Baltimore, there were four Pan-Hellenic sororities. The African American Pan-Hellenic Council coordinated efforts between the groups, combining their strength through unity. Founded in May 1930, the organization represented the nine African American Greek-lettered groups, five fraternities and four sororities. The fraternities were Alpha Phi Alpha, Omega Psi Phi, Kappa Alpha Psi, Phi Beta Sigma and Iota Phi Theta, the youngest, joining in 1996. The sororities were Alpha Kappa Alpha, Delta Sigma Theta, Zeta Phi Beta and Sigma Gamma Rho. According to its website, the organization sought to bring "unanimity of thought and action as far as possible" toward creating harmony on social, political and economic interests of African Americans. Victorine joined one Pan-Hellenic sorority and two professional sororities. All three sororities' principal aims were education and empowerment.

The oldest of the three Victorine joined was Sigma Gamma Rho. Sigma was founded on November 12, 1922, in Indianapolis, Indiana. The founders were Mary Lou Allison Gardner Little, Dorothy Hanley Whiteside, Vivian White Marbury, Nannie Mae Johnson, Hattie Mae Annette Dulin Redford, Bessie Mae Downey Rhoades Martin and Cubena McClure. All seven became teachers and/or school administrators. Victorine joined Alpha Alpha Sigma chapter. Through Sigma, Victorine organized fundraisers, contributed to scholarships and cross-fertilized her other organizations by inviting them to join her NCNW and CWDCC groups. The women of Sigma held values that encouraged sisterhood, respect and integrity. In July 1969, Victorine was the honorary chairman of the Rhomania Cotillion. The theme, "You—Our How for Tomorrow," informed the young women that violence was not a solution to racial intolerance. Education and the vote were the most effective tools. Victorine wanted them to be prepared for coming opportunities. Victorine said, "Study and be prepared for tomorrow's tasks of building a better world in which to live and work." The Rhoers were a junior division of young women being mentored by Sigma members. The Rhomania Pageant afforded young women an opportunity to learn and hone skills that would be useful in adult life as educated, professional women. Sigma also organized an adult affiliate, the Philos, made up of adult women with associate degrees or a record of matriculating at a four-year institution. The collective portrait of African American women fueled Victorine with being able to realize an aspect of her desire to maintain persistent vigilance and information transfer between women. Also in 1969, at the thirty-second Boule (national meeting), Grand Basileus Dr. Lorraine A. Williams set the conference tone as one of active engagement. Dr. Williams was the first woman to serve as the vice president of academic affairs for Howard University. She also served as the national program chairwoman for the NCNW and convened a nationwide interracial conference. Dr. Williams noted that "social organizations are no longer relevant unless they relate to the needs of their communities." Toward this end, there was a panel of politics that included Mississippi civil rights activist Fannie Lou Hamer, Dr. Tilman Cothran of Atlanta University's Sociology Department and Victorine. The panel spoke on political action and the need to increase political awareness.

The second sorority, Phi Delta Kappa, was founded on May 23, 1923, in Jersey City, New Jersey. In March 1923, at Jersey City Normal School, Dr. Gladys Merrit Ross gathered several teachers together to discuss the formation of a sorority. Those in attendance agreed, and PDK was born. Along with Dr. Ross were Julia Asbury Barnes, Dr. Florence Steele Hunt, Dr. Gladys Cannon Nunery, Ella Wells Butler, Mildred Morris Williams, Edna

Above: Dorothea Towles announcing a Charm Center fashion show, November 12, 1955. Towles was the first successful African American fashion model in Paris, France. A college graduate who majored in biology and pre-med, she traveled to France in 1949 and started modeling. She was selected by Christian Dior to fill in for a regular model, after which her career blossomed. *Victorine Quille Adams papers, Box 12-15, folder 15. Courtesy of the Beulah M. Davis Special Collections, Morgan State University.*

Right: Victorine and fashion model Dorothea Towles at the Charm Center, 1955. *Victorine Quille Adams papers, Box 12-15, folder 15. Courtesy of the Beulah M. Davis Special Collections, Morgan State University.*

McConnell and Marguerite Gross. Their principal aim was to promote the higher ideals of the teaching profession. Victorine joined Gamma Chapter. In 1951, PDK sought to link the formative years for children and peace. The continued threat of war disturbed children's developmental growth. To lessen the impact, Gamma Chapter furnished Lexington Street recreation center. The solution to the waning attention to segregated city services was being met through women and members of PDK. Annual contributions were made by every chapter to a scholarship award to assist a graduating female student who desired a career in teaching. The sorors also maintained a library in Monrovia, Liberia. The collection of 1,900 books continued to grow through donations of cash and books. The basileus (president) of Gamma Chapter in 1951 was Delores C. Hunt. Dr. Hunt graduated from Morgan State and ultimately served on the board of trustees. She served on the board of visitors for Coppin State and the board of the Baltimore City Teachers Union. She retired from teaching as a school principal.

The third sorority Victorine was involved in was Iota Phi Lambda, founded in 1929 by Lola Mercedes Parker. Iota worked to encourage young women to enter into business in tandem with formal business education/training. Parker was an administrative professional. She worked with Chicago congressman Arthur W. Mitchell and served as the first African American department manager at R.H. Donnelley Corporation. Parker connected Iota to NCNW and Bethune's vast network of women's clubs. Moreover, Parker's desire to see African American businesswomen connected would provide the best classroom through sharing strategies and techniques across generational and state lines.

In 1956, Victorine was honored by Iota Phi Lambda as Woman of the Year. Alice F. Ford, of Phi Delta Kappa, in writing about Victorine stated:

> *Prior to her affiliation with the Charm Center, Victorine Q. Adams distinguished herself as an "outstanding" teacher in the Baltimore Public School System. Because of her exceptional performance in the classroom…in later years when [Victorine] decided to enter the field of business, the interest, enthusiasm and efficiency which she displayed in the classroom were transferred to her new vocation. Because of her competent management, her exquisite taste, and her overpowering energy, the Charm Center exemplifies its name in every sense of the word. It is truly a "center of charm" patronized by all ladies who would be "chic." Through the promotional efforts of [Victorine], the Charm Center's "Fashion Show" has become popular among fraternal and civic organizations as a money*

Iota Phi Lambda group picture celebrating Victorine's being named Woman of the Year, 1956. Photo by Smith. *Victorine Quille Adams papers, Box 12-15, folder 5. Courtesy of the Beulah M. Davis Special Collections, Morgan State University.*

raising enterprise. Time, talent and use of facilities are given gratis to all organizations having a charitable purpose. By this unique method, Mrs. Adams not only advertises the Charm Center, but she also establishes good public relations through rendering an unselfish and civic service. Therefore, it is the sincere wish of the National Sorority of Phi Delta Kappa, Gamma Chapter that Iota Phi Lambda Sorority at its 1956 National Convention will find it feasible to bestow upon our beloved soror, Mrs. Victorine Q. Adams, the title "MOST OUTSTANDING BUSINESS WOMAN OF THE YEAR."[48]

The recognition of excellent service in the community enriched many lives in Baltimore. The fashion shows modeled clothing and styles for local women, while the facilities served as an additional meeting place for the CWDCC and Woman Power. The location's dual purpose speaks to unique aspects of being an African American woman activist during the mid-twentieth century. A clothing boutique, while innocuous in appearance, gave these women a space to embrace their whole selves—brains, beauty and sensibility. It also afforded sales associates, often younger women, the

Dorothea Towles, *right*, and Baltimore city teachers at the Charm Center, November 1955. *Victorine Quille Adams papers, Box 12-15, folder 15. Courtesy of the Beulah M. Davis Special Collections, Morgan State University.*

opportunity to mingle with mature women, while also allowing Baltimoreans to encounter Ella Fitzgerald, Billie Holiday and Dorothea Towles, notable women they read about in *Ebony* and *JET* magazines.

The overlapping interests and intersections between African American professionals contributed to the success of Victorine's CWDCC and her future Woman Power, Incorporated. The sorors knew that their task was herculean and required all efforts to propel the race forward. Everything from the local conditions of city schools to the national issues on public accommodations impacted the quality of life for future generations. These women were aware of the sacrifices made to provide them with a good education, clean housing, safe streets and viable careers. As stewards, it was imperative for them to improve conditions for all women. Victorine's success resided in keeping herself connected and focused on civic issues that impacted equity and access to Baltimore residents from living fully actualized lives. Through her membership in these organizations, she realized others were working toward similar goals and all experiences were life lessons, whether good or bad.

Chapter 4

GRASSROOTS POLITICS

Taking Authority in the Streets

T he decision in *Brown v. Board of Education* coupled with increasing numbers
of registered voters signaled a change in the country. Concurrently,
black college students demonstrated against segregation in all forms
throughout the South. Life for black Baltimoreans slowly improved. Morgan
students orchestrated protest measures in the Northwood Shopping Center.
Their strategies were honed through measured tactics and coordinating
with established civil rights groups such as the NAACP. The generations
of accomplished Morgan alums now occupied professions and political
offices coupled with fraternal/sorority relationships, and this emboldened
the students to crusade for justice. The majority of the student population
hailed from Baltimore or counties throughout Maryland, so their fight was
not simply an exercise in civil disobedience but a demand to live as full
American citizens. Throughout the 1940s, male and some female students
served in World War II, and later, others participated in the Korean War.
The fight for democracy abroad rang hollow in the ears of these veterans
who risked their lives and lost friends to defend an ideal they could not fully
enjoy as Americans. From Annapolis in 1941 to Northwood Theater in 1955,
Morgan students responded to unfair treatment, at times accompanied by
white college students.

Therefore, opting to attend Morgan further radicalized students when
basic resources such as a gymnasium and adequate funding for academic
programs remained underfunded or experienced gross delays in state
funding being received. Morgan's existence throughout the twentieth

century was a battle of will, wits and legal action that reaffirmed in the minds of the campus community the need to consistently organize and demand change perpetually from generation to generation. Morgan president Dr. Martin D. Jenkins walked a fine line in attempts to secure funding and grow the college. Nevertheless, he utilized the college curriculum to craft students into informed and dynamic global citizens whose educational instruction would contribute to desperately needed solutions. Jenkins envisioned Morgan as a place where men and women graduated with the ability to think clearly, read with understanding and convey ideas in written and oral fashion with an awareness of American history and human compassion. Jenkins said students need "[t]o have a passion for the democratic way of life; to have courage of [their] convictions, the desire and willingness to 'stand up and be counted' for those things in which [they] believe."[49] He said, "Although the task of improving the general level of the Negro population is not wholly an educational one, it is partly so. Whatever the college can do in this regard, we propose to do....We intend to constitute a channel of communication in racial matters and to promote harmonious race relations within the state and nation."[50] Toward this end, Morgan opened the Institute for Political Education in 1959 and Urban Studies Institute in 1964. The institutes' primary focus placed academic theory in real-time problems plaguing Baltimore, allowing research-based solutions to those problems. This connection to scholarship and the community further sensitized the student population to the depth of social ills. This link was further strengthened by Morgan alums throughout Baltimore, where students and faculty were welcomed. During his administration from 1948 to 1970, Jenkins fought through the scholarly environment he cultivated and through exposing students to applied scholarship through the institutes.

This evolving ideological and political climate provided a fertile seedbed for Victorine and her numerous women's organizations. Though blacks were increasingly educated, established and connected, with access to funding and sponsorship, injustice and discrimination did not completely stop; however, those in favor of the status quo faced a foe determined to expose, root out and demolish hateful practices in all areas of life.

ALL POLITICS ARE LOCAL:
PROVIDENT HOSPITAL AND THE BARRETT SCHOOL

The health and wellness of African Americans was challenging in Baltimore. The segregated medical facilities provided medical attention. The larger opportunity to meet the community's needs included African American doctors and nurses, but unfortunately, racism precluded the hospitals from allowing integrated medical staffing. In response, African Americans opened their own medical schools and teaching and fully functioning hospitals. Provident Hospital was established in June 1894 with ten beds at 419 Orchard Street in northwest Baltimore. Provident opened with the intention to fulfill three aims: to offer a place where black Baltimoreans were able to be treated by black physicians; to offer a place where black medical professionals were able to train; and to organize a nursing program. Within one year, it had expanded and moved to West Biddle Street, with another building attached to the main facility. Challenged with maintenance issues, Provident was always fundraising to mend and improve its facilities. This was in part from receiving "little to no money" from the state or city government. Within the first ten years, Baltimore stopped all funding, while Maryland continued to make paltry donations. Burdened with great financial challenges, the pioneers clung to their three-fold mission.

During Provident's infancy, women were principally involved in fundraising efforts. The Ladies Board of Managers assisted in every way possible to ensure that Provident remained open. From 1914 to 1925, Provident considered relocation to meet the demand. It innovated a postgraduate training program for young doctors and received donations from empathetic whites. According to the *Afro* in 1927, the most successful fundraising campaign netted $425,000. Principal donors were black Baltimoreans, who raised $165,000; whites, $149,000; $25,000 apiece from the Rosenwald Fund and Rockefeller Foundation; and various gifts totaling $100,000. In October 1928, the new Provident Hospital and Free Dispensary opened at 1514 Division Street. The new building, designed by African American architect Albert C. Cassell, housed new equipment and internal spaces conducive to modern medical practice needs. The tumultuous 1930s contributed to existing challenges Provident knew all too well; however, its excellent medical treatment for African Americans morphed into a national example that raised funds and its value in Baltimore. Rosenwald and Rockefeller suggested other cities with majority/large black populations visit Provident and replicate its success throughout the country.

In 1967, construction of the new 280-bed hospital was begun. A Maryland voter referendum decided to grant Provident $2.4 million in state funds to match funds secured by the hospital. What began as one building with 10 beds in 1894 by 1967 had relocated to a 22.5-acre campus. The explosive growth was not without straining challenges. Victorine served on the Provident Hospital Development Committee. In the spirit of the Ladies Board of Managers, Victorine and other women—and some men—sought to solicit gifts through a door-to-door campaign seeking any and all sizes of financial donations. In tandem with fundraising, in true Victorine fashion, she organized a "get out the vote" campaign for a new Provident Hospital in October 1962. One direct mailer proclaimed:

> *We need your talent and experience on the Citizens Committee for a New Provident Hospital. Our series task is defined in two areas:*
> *Area I—To get out a majority Vote for the Hospital Loan and*
> *Area II—To raise our quota of money for the new hospital*
> *Without success in Area I, there can be no second stage of our project. In Area I, the situation is serious—TO GET OUT THE VOTE FOR THE HOSPITAL LOAN!*
> *We need dedicated people to hold down important positions and get positive results, so you have been considered:*
> *First: As a Precinct Specialist to work in your block, to get your neighbors to vote for the New Provident Hospital Loan.*
> *Second: To get other people to work in their blocks to help the cause.*
> *Please accept this important and necessary responsibility. Please sign and return this letter. WE NEED YOU!*[51]

This direct mailer circulated among all of Victorine's affiliate organizations. Access to healthcare was critical for African Americans with limited resources; it was the thin line between life and death. Provident hobbled along throughout the 1970s and 1980s. African Americans raised $1 million, far exceeding their goal of $60,000. The 1980s and the chilling effect of Reaganism threw the needs of the working urban poor to charitable organizations. Moreover, the fickle relationship of race and class in Baltimore signaled the demise of Provident Hospital. By 1986, Provident had merged with Lutheran Hospital, becoming Liberty. In 1996, attempts to save Liberty proposed a merger with Bon Secours Hospital. The proposed merger anticipated a move in the right direction to save the hospital, then located in the Mondawmin complex. Unfortunately, by the 1990s, the needs of patients were shifting from standard medical emergencies to incidents stemming from drug and mental health challenges. A Maryland Health Resources Planning Commission study explored the income level of those within the hospital's zip code. The average income was $9,920 a year, which is equivalent to $15,900 in 2018. The root cause of medical problems was not considered, coupled with the underutilized facility; of the 280+ beds, only 90 were occupied most of the time. In 1999, Liberty Hospital closed, and all patients transferred or referred to Bon Secours, three miles away.

The closure of Liberty marked a shift away from the golden age of African American self-help and beneficial private-public partnership. On June 30, 2000, Victorine wrote an article for the *Afro*, "Provident Hospital: The Tearing Down of a Legacy." In this piece, she grieved the loss of Provident as a resource and symbol. She lamented the "lost hopes" of those progenitors of Provident, the known and unknown persons who sacrificed, fought and donated to this grand vision of African American healthcare and training. This loss was personal for her because she had championed the cause of Provident through contributing her human resources to keeping the doors open. Victorine noted:

> *It was a struggle to get legislation passed in Annapolis to continue the progress. It was a struggle to fire up the community to the task. When all that legwork was done, the biggest struggle was raising matching funds. The whole city rallied behind Charles Tildon to get the project funding underway. The late Max Johnson, of the [Afro] challenged Woman Power, Inc., founded by me, then Councilwoman, and Ethel P. Rich in 1958 to pull its weight in that direction. Dr. Delores C. Hunt urged Woman Power, Inc. to take a leadership role in the project under the Women's Division. Dr. Hunt spearheaded the drive. Woman Power, Inc. organized the Century Club, made up of more than 100 women dedicated to contribute or raise $100 each within a year. The goal was $10,000. The quota was raised on time. Woman Power, Inc. held a raffle. Anderson Chevrolet donated a brand new yellow four-door Chevrolet with a reversible top. The raffle was a success. F. Ballantine and Sons sponsored a golf tournament with the entire proceeds donated. [The events featured] Joe Louis, the World's Heavyweight Champion and Marguerite Bellafonte, the beautiful actress. At the same time, fraternities, sororities, women's clubs, church groups all bonded together and struggled to reach their goals. The whole city—Black, White, rich, poor, all cultures, men's clubs and businessmen—worked together to raise funds for [Provident].[52]*

Charles Tildon speaking at Democratic Women at the Adamses' home on Carlisle Avenue. Seated to Tildon's right is Morgan State professor G. James Fleming. Tildon was a Baltimore educator and civic activist who believed in community engagement. He championed local causes from Provident Hospital to racial and religious tolerance. *Victorine Quille Adams papers, Box 12-15, folder 1. Courtesy of the Beulah M. Davis Special Collections, Morgan State University.*

The community interest and private donations worked to keep the doors open and the state made matching contributions; however, the disinvestment in urban poor marked an end to the focus of local government. Derelict neighborhoods were severed from the intentions of 1990s urban planning. Throughout the country, drug addiction was criminalized and the underclass faulted for being underachieving, the walking wounded. Children and elderly were swept aside into the margins, out of sight, out of mind and without a loud voice in city/state government. Of note in her article, Victorine inquired about the historical materials that composed Provident's existence, the documents, artifacts and photographs. Once the building was razed, the tangible history would be the only record of its having been in Baltimore. The records were slated to arrive at Morgan, but after discussion, the collection was deposited at the Baltimore City Archives, while other

Left to right, back row: Sarah Lamb, Geneva Griffin, Vera Gill, John Ashly and Bud Hosford. *Front row:* Blanche Gales, Edith Stevens and Victorine. This Woman Power, Incorporated raffle was a fundraiser for Provident Hospital. *Victorine Quille Adams papers, Box 12-14, folder 11. Courtesy of the Beulah M. Davis Special Collections, Morgan State University.*

items are located at the Maryland Historical Society. Victorine concluded, "I will cry and I will fall apart—completely. However, the grief, the rage, and the sorrow will not deter the Big Ball. It's a shame."[53]

Another crusade for Victorine was the welfare and well-being of girls, especially those with the odds stacked against them. The Barrett Training School for Colored Girls opened in 1882 as a facility for "colored" girls without proper supervision. These were orphans, delinquent or wayward girls for whom the state claimed responsibility, thus housing and providing for their basic needs. The girls were minors and therefore could not provide for themselves and were seemingly without families or community agencies to attend to their needs. Several facilities akin to the Barrett School existed for white boys and girls and "colored" boys. In light of their voicelessness from age, race and class, these girls faced mounting prejudice and abuse. In 1931, President Herbert Hoover organized the Wickersham Commission to investigate the conditions of these facilities. Three sites in Maryland were cited for subpar conditions. The Barrett Training School for Colored Girls on Conduit Road reported young mothers infected with venereal disease without adequate medical treatment. The National Training School for White Girls at Muirkirk and the National Training School for Boys on Bladenburg Road were severely criticized. The report condemned the federal government for lack of regulations concerning these types of facilities yet recommended that the state implement better programming. The African American girls were "locked in" at night, even though the windows were barred or covered with heavy wire grating. The girls attended three hours of classroom instruction in the winter and none in the autumn. There was no gymnasium or recreation. There was no medical staff onsite, and a visiting physician attended the girls twice a week. Punishment and daily ritual, according to the commission, were medieval in fashion. The girls were subject to flogging, shackling, marching or dressing "to a count," as well as enduring strenuous standing in position. The commission's report brought about enforced segregation and meager improvements in white facilities.

Victorine was appointed to the Barrett Training School for Colored Girls by Governor Herbert O'Connor in 1946 and remained there for ten years. During her tenure, she worked to improve resources for the girls. To stimulate their minds, she engaged them as if she were in her classroom. In Victorine's mind, their potential was not reduced to their location. Some girls were victims of grinding poverty brought about by the Depression. Some parents placed their children in facilities where they would be fed and housed. Within six years, Victorine was put in charge of educational programming. In this position, she assisted girls with academic instruction to qualify for high schools when released or collected by family members. Victorine negotiated with a middle and high school to admit the girls who remained housed on campus. This enrichment equipped the girls to walk into adulthood educated with basic skills needed to obtain jobs to provide for themselves.

On January 13, 1956, Joseph Sterne wrote an article, "Integrating Delinquents Is Ruled Out," in the *Sun* about an early effort to integrate the facilities that was shot down by Maryland attorney general C. Ferdinand Sybert. Sybert argued that in the absence of a "clear indication that a decision of our courts or of the Supreme Court, invalidates a given statue, we must withhold condemnation of the law." The decision in *Brown v. Board of Education*, in his opinion, was narrow and not applicable to other state laws that supported segregation. Governor Theodore McKeldin hoped "that we might be able to carry out the same program [of desegregation] in the training schools as in the public schools." Howard H. Murphy of the State Board of Public Welfare disagreed with Sybert. Murphy went further to note that "the Supreme Court's [decision] nullified segregation in the training schools and it was [Sybert's duty] to so rule." Segregation was expensive in maintaining a dual system; therefore, integration would better serve the taxpayers. Sybert cosigned an opinion of Norman P. Ramsey, deputy attorney, that relegated the training schools to a "unique position" when placed beside public schools. Unrelenting, Sybert concluded that it was not the state's function to make policy in this area. To him, the separate branches of government should not encroach upon one another.

During the squabble among state legislators, Victorine continued her work with the girls, expanding their exposure to elements of home training neglected while at Barrett's. Her charm courses worked to inform the young women about deportment, dress and poise. The stigma attached to poverty rivaled that of color, but she believed their "handicap" did not mean that they could not rise above their current station in life. The vast network of women's clubs and coterie of teachers and social workers enabled Victorine to connect these girls with viable resources. Victorine's work had a patina of Christian ministry to the less fortunate, exemplified by the Oblates and Catholic charities throughout Baltimore. Toward that end, many middle-class African Americans were connected to Christian faith traditions. Unfortunately, at times ugly encounters along complexion and class lines soured relationships and tacitly excluded groups of black women who did not "fit" within the cultured aesthetic of a particular group. Victorine knew well the obstacles that faced these girls, and she worked hard to ensure that they were confident, equipped and aware that they could become productive members of society.

In 1959, the NAACP filed suit on behalf of the four training schools. The suit was filed by Tucker R. Dearing on behalf of taxpayers who maintained that segregated training schools was contrary to the *Brown* decision. Stemming from the vocal indifference of Sybert, the NAACP argued the merits of the *Brown* decision did, in fact, apply to the segregated training schools. If the schools were to be integrated, what campus would be closed? The final decision closed the Barrett School campus, and the residents relocated to the Montrose School. This decision took six years before it was implemented. The integration saved millions of dollars of state funds. The 1960s further broadened the possibilities for black Baltimoreans. Progressive whites worked as best as possible with African Americans, yet the specter of race lingered as whites witnessed and experienced a new generation of black Baltimoreans. This new generation was vocal, organized and physically engaged. They used all available methods to dismantle segregation and level the playing field. They were young and old people, high school and university students, black, white and other. Using direct-action protests to lunch counter sit-ins to possible arrest, the new generation pushed for integration and equity in Maryland. As America convulsed, colonized countries throughout the world shook off aged manacles, simultaneously claiming their independence wrapped up in ethnic pride and neo-nationalism. As the world stage acknowledged the newly formed countries, women were also seeking a place in world affairs. The 1960s would be the time Baltimore would make new history for African American women.

Co-Founding Woman Power, Incorporated: Ethel P. Rich and Integration

In May 1958, Victorine received a giant tribute for her contributions to political education and voter registration. A testimonial banquet given in honor held at Morgan State celebrated her as "one of the city's most powerful Democratic women organizers." Her CWDCC had reconfigured the voting structure of Baltimore's black community. Her organization wrested power from black male politicians and openly challenged the Jack Pollack political boss empire. An impressive 350 people attended the banquet, representing all aspects of Victorine's influence, from family to friends to politicians. Congressman George H. Fallon applauded her efforts in representing Baltimore in Washington, D.C. It was remarked that Victorine embodied intelligence and a selfless devotion to Baltimore. Lillie M. Jackson noted that her interest in the welfare of others was the mark of a public servant. Lloyd Randolph remarked on her magnetic ability. Her pioneering endeavor into voter registration appealed to women and kept them interested, active and involved.

It is no surprise that the seeds sown in May 1958 blossomed that summer. On August 19, 1958, the concept of Woman Power, Incorporated, arrived on the Baltimore scene. This group would be national in scope, functioning throughout America and subject to the rules and regulations of Woman Power, Incorporated–National, located in Baltimore. The three aims of Woman Power were to mobilize black women for political action and power; to mobilize black women for community involvement; and to mobilize black women for educational commitment. Political action took the form of voter registration of the individual and everyone within her respective sphere of influence. Moreover, it required that Election Day was the focus of the membership—getting people to the polls, as well as teaching and learning about the process, candidates and governance of state regulations. The final aim of political action would be to gain political control of our communities and elect qualified black women and men. Community involvement examined political issues and questions on the ballot. Members would learn and educate others on the impact and effect of proposed matters with regard to how those decisions improved or neglected the black community. Each question or measure—be it relating to building a new school, redistricting Baltimore or constructing an expressway—needed to be studied, evaluated and explained, empowering every member and audience with sound information to ensure that the black community benefited from the best outcome. This relied on the principle of "each one teach one," making the most impact through the ballot box. Finally, education was essential to demystifying the political process.

Victorine co-founded Woman Power with Ethel P. Rich. The two most likely encountered each other through work with Provident Hospital. Rich worked at Provident from 1933 to 1942. In April 1942, she was dismissed as an admitting officer and social worker. She sued, disputing the reason. A supervisor accused Rich of insubordination and ordered her from the hospital. After being verbally accosted, Rich was promptly removed from her job. Rich charged that the treatment she received was unfounded, deprived her of an income, besmirched her character and impeded her ability to work in her chosen profession. In August 1942, Rich, with her attorney present, entered a plea for damages of $1,000 and for the recovery of back wages of $450. Rich testified that she had worked for nine years without incident and her dismissal was wrongful and unjust. An all-white jury found Rich's claims unfounded. The supervisor's testimony accused Rich of numerous acts of insubordination, yet none of the hospital administrators were aware or had documentation to confirm the supervisor's accusations. As a result, Rich did not return to Provident, and four board members resigned in protest to the despotic tyranny of the supervisor. There is no additional information from the *Afro* regarding Rich's post-trial employment. Nevertheless, she partnered with Victorine and employed her training in social work and administration to create an organization that would shift Maryland politics.

Woman Power was nonpartisan and sought to educate women about the political process. Seminars were held in familiar spaces—churches, schools and municipal buildings—for all people, youth and adults. Woman Power purchased a voting machine to allow the educational experience to become tactile. The instructional automatic voting machine, Jamestown, New York model #4377, was donated with Victorine's collection to Morgan.

The motto of Woman Power was "each one reach one, each one teach one," thus diffusing leadership and allowing all people to learn and participate according to their comfort level and neighborhood. This was strategic because women educated their children and shared with their husbands, which allowed the information the widest possible audience through an established channel of sharing. Woman Power publicly supported state measures that would equalize educational opportunities across Maryland. Victorine credited two men for helping her realize Woman Power: Dr. Carl J. Murphy, publisher of the *Afro American* newspaper, and Dr. Willard J. Allen, Most Worshipful Grand Master of the Prince Hall Masons of Maryland. Murphy inherited the *Afro* from his father, who started the paper in the 1890s. Murphy taught German at Howard University and grew the circulation of the *Afro*. He served as the first African American chairman of the board of trustees at Morgan during the Jenkins administration. Allen served as president of Southern Life Insurance Company and owner of W.W. Real Estate Company. He served the Prince Hall Masons as the most puissant sovereign grand commander for thirty-two years. He also served as a trustee at Morgan State for twenty-two years. His two daughters were Baltimore schoolteachers. These men understood the importance of Victorine's work on behalf of the race and supported her efforts.

Woman Power membership was open to all women, regardless of their occupation. They believed that every woman could teach something and every woman could learn something. There was no party affiliation, but every member was required to be a registered voter. Men were welcome to join the Minute Men and contribute in unique ways throughout Baltimore. The Minute Men drove cars, donated services and money and offered manual support. Additional funds were generated by donations and dues. Regular membership was $10 a year. Contributing members paid $25, and donors paid $50 a year. Angel members paid $100+. All members selected

CWDCC voter registration. Ethel Rich is at the far left, and Ruth Turner is at the far right. Photo by Brown. *Victorine Quille Adams papers, Box 12-15, folder 4. Courtesy of the Beulah M. Davis Special Collections, Morgan State University.*

a subcommittee to work with; the categories were education, community and political areas. According to an undated membership brochure, Woman Power refined its aims to disseminate political information, direct political action on community issues and stimulate an awareness of the importance of the ballot for economic, social and civic progress. To accomplish these aims, it maintained ongoing workshops to address issues affecting all citizens; conducted voter registration drives encouraging all citizens to accept the right and privilege of voting; examined political issues on local affairs; and finally, members traveled to the General Assembly in Annapolis, as well as city and county council sessions.

The organizational structure included president/director, first vice president, second vice president, third vice president, corresponding secretary, recording secretary, assistant recording secretary, financial secretary, treasurer, assistant treasurer, chaplain, historian and field secretary. A parliamentarian would be appointed by the president. To qualify for an office, the member needed to be active and in good financial standing for two years, attend a minimum of two-thirds of the

Victorine, Mrs. Samuel K. Himmelrich and Bernice White at a Woman Power event, October 31, 1965. *Victorine Quille Adams papers, Box 12-15, folder 10. Courtesy of the Beulah M. Davis Special Collections, Morgan State University.*

regular monthly meetings the year preceding a bid for office and have served as a committee chairman. One of the earliest administrations was Dr. Delores C. Hunt, president; Erla McKinnon, vice president; Betty L. Warren, recording secretary; Lillian Tate, corresponding secretary; Lillian M. Dorsey, financial secretary; Hortense Henry, treasurer; Vera LeCato, assistant treasurer; Victorine, research director; Florence Kidd, program coordinator; Bernice S. White, field secretary; Ethel P. Rich, director of public affairs. In attempts to reduce crime, Woman Power invited Violet Hill Whyte to serve as a consultant to the Crime Committee. Whyte was the first African American female police officer in Baltimore. Appointed in 1937, she was respected throughout the black community. She earned the moniker "Lady Law" in part from performing her function as a police officer. A graduate of Coppin State and formerly a schoolteacher, Whyte was aware of the root causes of criminal activity and sought to prevent activities from escalating. During her thirty-year career, she never had to

Gladys Barbour, Victorine and Ruth Turner of Woman Power, Inc. I. Henry Philip photograph. *Victorine Quille Adams papers, Box 12-15, folder 8. Courtesy of the Beulah M. Davis Special Collections, Morgan State University.*

CWDCC Minute Men, *left to right*: Sydnor (last name not listed), William White, Caesar Jones, James Morris and Dallas Davis. Photo by Brown. *Victorine Quille Adams papers, Box 12-15, folder 4. Courtesy of the Beulah M. Davis Special Collections, Morgan State University.*

fire her weapon and was credited as being humane, even within Baltimore law enforcement. When she joined the Crime Committee, she was retired from the police department, and crime shifted within the black community; however, human nature and needs remained the same, and addressing the root of problems worked best for Whyte and Woman Power.

In 1959, Woman Power held its second leadership conference. The theme was "Knowledge and Action in Registering to Vote." The first leadership conference was held on September 21, 1958. This event effectively integrated the Sheraton Belvedere Hotel. The speakers at the second conference hailed from across the Eastern Seaboard. Polly Weeden, the national president of the Links, addressed the "crop of femmes" with encouraging words, saying that we need "more work" and less talk. Dr. Lorraine Williams of Sigma Gamma Rho noted that we cannot depend on politics alone; we must know the power of the vote and the strength voting numbers has on all aspects of public policy. Victorine did not miss an

Ethel P. Rich (*second from left*) at a Woman Power leadership luncheon. To the left of Rich is Dr. Delores Hunt. It is believed that the Woman Power luncheon integrated the Belvedere Hotel in Baltimore in 1958. *Victorine Quille Adams papers, Box 12-15, folder 8. Courtesy of the Beulah M. Davis Special Collections, Morgan State University.*

Victorine is to the right of the podium and Dr. Martin D. Jenkins and Dr. G. James Fleming are to her left at a Woman Power leadership luncheon. *Victorine Quille Adams papers, Box 12-15, folder 8. Courtesy of the Beulah M. Davis Special Collections, Morgan State University.*

opportunity to share chic fashions from the Charm Center. Woman Power themed its conferences to reflect the changes and challenges to its aims of educating and electing black women. In 1963, the theme was "The Power of Woman Power"; in 1966, "A Time for Action Woman Power and the Ballot Box"; and in 1970, "Direct Action on the Local Level." On Sunday, October 22, 1967, Mayor Theodore McKeldin designated Woman Power Day. McKeldin declared:

> *Woman Power Incorporated has been in the forefront in the political life of this City for a decade.*
>
> *Woman Power Incorporated has been dedicated to the objective of educating and organizing women for political action.*
>
> *Woman Power Incorporated has recognized the responsibility to give service to the Provident Hospital Development Fund to assist financially toward the new health facility.*

Left to right: Victorine, Dr. Delores C. Hunt and Ethel P. Rich with other women at a Woman Power luncheon, circa 1950s. *Victorine Quille Adams papers, Box 12-15, folder 8. Courtesy of the Beulah M. Davis Special Collections, Morgan State University.*

> *Woman Power Incorporated is observing a decade of progress at the Tenth Annual Luncheon and Workshop.*
> *NOW, THEREFORE, I THEODORE R. MCKELDIN, MAYOR of the City of Baltimore, do hereby proclaim Sunday, October 22, 1967 as "WOMAN POWER DAY" in Baltimore.*[54]

Woman Power benefited from Victorine's classroom administration. She produced numerous pamphlets, newsletters and phone trees to reinforce the structural order of Woman Power. In 1968, a proposed registration program to get out the vote for Hubert Humphrey crafted by Victorine and Ethel was distributed to the membership. The dual effort would increase Negro registration and increase the number of voting Negroes on Election Day. Victorine listed the precincts needing special attention and listed the black organizations that needed to be informed of the "why" in considering Humphrey. To accomplish this goal, Woman Power would staff and operate

Left to right: Ethel P. Rich, William Donald Schafer and Victorine receiving a proclamation for Woman Power, Incorporated on October 22, 1967. *Victorine Quille Adams papers, Box 12-9, folder 3. Courtesy of the Beulah M. Davis Special Collections, Morgan State University.*

an office at the cost of $6,000. The office help included messengers, office assistants, office equipment, a janitor and a street team. The emphasis would be on block captains and precinct participation. The women informed the membership that this campaign was directly anti-Wallace. Humphrey won the Democratic nomination but lost the presidential election to Richard M. Nixon. He returned to the Senate and died eight years later.

In another pamphlet, the women offered some suggestive *how-to*s in area registering and getting out the vote. In this pamphlet, Victorine chronicled the successes of the CWDCC, which existed alongside Woman Power and lived just as long, well into the 1990s. Using the radio and newspapers to stimulate conversation among black people, she impressed upon them the need to exert consistent interest in politics, even when no election is scheduled to occur. She sought to remind them that political issues rise out of needs or demands from the government or citizens. Through making voter education an element of the consumer culture, political issues

Kwesi Mfume (*center*) at the Colored Women's Democratic Campaign Committee annual banquet. *Victorine Quille Adams papers, Box 12-15, folder 1. Courtesy of the Beulah M. Davis Special Collections, Morgan State University.*

become familiar and not mysterious and foreign. She instructed members to scour popular places, such as taverns, busy corners, schools, union halls and churches. These methods worked to empower black people as informed and dynamic partners in the process of politics and no longer objects of political convenience. In 1971, Woman Power had chapters in several counties throughout Maryland, as well as New York; Newark, New Jersey; Wilmington, Delaware; Washington, D.C.; and Detroit, Michigan.

BALTIMORE CITY AND THE NEW BLACK POLITICIAN

Victorine's endeavors with the CWDCC and Woman Power broadened the idea of what a politician did and looked like. This petite woman who left the elementary school classroom crafted a space for herself in the field of political education. Victorine's interests included mentoring younger people. Professor G. James Fleming, a political scientist from Morgan State, provided her opportunities to share the live experience of politics. Fleming was a native of St. Croix, U.S. Virgin Islands. He migrated to New York and obtained a public school education. He attended Hampton Institute, graduating in 1926. He obtained his doctorate in political science from the University of Pennsylvania in 1948. His personal and professional interests concerned equity and fair play. He joined the faculty at Morgan in 1954. The campus was ripe for his instruction, as political matters bubbled up as the NAACP crusaded to root out segregation laws. Through his efforts, Fleming secured a Ford Foundation grant of $103,000 that provided the seedbed for the Institute for Political Education at Morgan. The institute was to assist in developing citizen-politicians through educational instruction at Morgan. Fleming incorporated students, alumni, the community and politicians to participate in the workshops. Events included mock elections, grassroots activities and volunteering in live campaigns throughout Baltimore. The success of the institute resulted in the Ford Foundation extending the programming for another four years at an increased amount of $175,000. Fleming led the institute from 1959 to 1966. The visionary leadership and success resulted in the formation of the Department of Political Science. Many credited Fleming with positioning Morgan State in the national conversation on race, politics and education. As a result of the institute, Morgan students experienced great success in politics. Parren Mitchell, former congressman from Baltimore; James H. Gilliam, successful lawyer and civil rights activist; and Judge Robert M. Bell, former chief justice for the State of Maryland, were all students of Fleming's.

Another Morganite who benefited from Fleming's instruction was Verda Welcome. She served in the Maryland House of Delegates from 1959 to 1963 and became the first African American woman in United States history to serve as a state senator. She served in the Maryland State Senate from 1963 to 1982. Through efforts established by Victorine and donations from her husband, Willie, Verda galvanized a group of women dubbed Valiant Women, who canvassed the community in the Fourth District, passing out literature on her behalf. When she arrived at the General Assembly, she chipped away at racial obstacles. Her personal encounters with segregation would not be the law of Maryland but follow suit with the federal decision in *Brown v. Board of Education.* She also introduced legislation to dismantle laws that restricted access to Maryland's hotels and public places. To the benefit of Morgan, she led the legislative fight to change Morgan State College

Victorine (*second from the right*) standing next to Professor G. James Fleming with an unidentified group, possibly conducting a voter education session. *Victorine Quille Adams papers, Box 12-14, folder 9. Courtesy of the Beulah M. Davis Special Collections, Morgan State University.*

into Morgan State University. This move enhanced Morgan's academic prestige and state funding. She also drafted legislation that resulted in the formation of the Maryland Commission on African American History and Culture. The commission selected Morgan's Dr. Benjamin A. Quarles and Dr. Roland C. McConnell as the first administrative team that crafted the mission to excavate Maryland's black history. She also challenged age-old miscegenation laws that remained in Maryland law books.

The Institute for Political Education held at Morgan afforded students and politicians the opportunity to connect the theory to the practical regarding politics. Victorine shared numerous topics with the Morgan students through the 1960s. In April 1962, a one-day workshop focused on "Practical Politics for Busy Organization Women and Students." Victorine presented a lecture on "How to Get into Politics and How to Get Others into Politics," as the executive director of Woman Power. Through the institute, she was able to advertise and recruit for the CWDCC and Woman Power. In January 1971, Mayor Thomas J. D'Alesandro and City Councilwoman Adams discussed aspects of politics and government. Mayor D'Alesandro noted that there were a number of problems in Baltimore; however, they could be solved if the counties and city worked together. Victorine spoke on grassroots politics, covering her experience with meeting the needs of blacks in Baltimore. The *Afro* reported Victorine stating, "When the white political power structure did not listen to black people or when black politicians paid their women no mind, [I founded two organizations] to give black women some political power." Moreover, she was able to demonstrate the effect dress and appearance had on African American women in social settings. This aspect of African American women was reinforced at Morgan through Thelma Bando, the dean of women. In the tradition established by Lucy Slowe and the first generation of HBCU female deans, they impressed the need to maintain a well-groomed appearance as a standard, in part from

Victorine at Women's Fair—Women Together, January 22, 1975. *Victorine Quille Adams papers, Box 12-15, folder 6. Courtesy of the Beulah M. Davis Special Collections, Morgan State University.*

Left to right: Delegate Loyal Randolph, Senator Larry Young, Senator John Jeffries, Senator Michael Bowen Mitchell, Abner Lee, Senator Clarence M. Mitchell III, Ray Haysbert, Willie Adams and Sterling Paige; *front row*: Councilwoman Victorine Quille Adams. A.R. Snowden photographer. *Victorine Quille Adams papers, Box 12-14, folder 2. Courtesy of the Beulah M. Davis Special Collections, Morgan State University.*

Victorine (*second on the right*) standing with an unidentified group of children on the campaign trail. *Victorine Quille Adams papers, Box 12-14, folder 9. Courtesy of the Beulah M. Davis Special Collections, Morgan State University.*

being a living refutation of stereotypes, as well as an ambassador for the race and the women of the race.

Victorine situated African American women—no longer on the periphery—at the helm with men, whites and others interested in creating a humane society that provided for the less fortunate and allowed all residents access to a voice and audience to learn and share their political thoughts. The youth were included in her vision as residents; they were the future. To ensure that all of her efforts were not lost to a generation not fully aware of the intricacies of politics, she encouraged them and supported social events for them to grow into balanced, well-adjusted adults who would exercise compassion for their fellow man and woman.

Chapter 5

LESSONS LEARNED
AND TAUGHT

A Legacy in Baltimore

The steady progress made through collective work and planning seemed to fizzle in 1968, when urban unrest in the wake of Dr. King's assassination threatened to undo most of the progress. Many of the political achievements were in tandem with race pride for African Americans. Unlike the struggle to integrate the training schools, public schools in Baltimore integrated with little trouble. However, within ten years, many of the schools had resegregated, in part from white flight, leaving black students under principally white teachers and administrators. Racism plagued pockets of Baltimore, and the underlying causes of poverty were never fully eradicated or addressed but bubbled over in an emotional cauldron that resulted in arson, looting and violence. The increase of heroin usage spiked criminal activities, from drug sales to robberies and medical emergencies. Governor Spiro T. Agnew sent the National Guard to Baltimore and imposed an 11:00 p.m. curfew. Agnew's insensitive comments confirmed white suspicions about the urban dweller fanning embers of racial indifference.

In *Black Social Capital: The Politics of School Reform in Baltimore, 1986–1998*, Marion Orr draws parallels between access to education and racial division within the city and indicates that Baltimore was a prosperous city attracting manufacturing businesses. From the 1920s through the 1950s, a series of diverse industries such as McCormick Spice, Proctor and Gamble, Western Electric, Bethlehem Steel and others provided for semi-skilled workers the ability to work jobs that provided a reasonable living. Many of these jobs were occupied by African American workers, some of whom migrated from Virginia and North Carolina looking for employment. However, Orr notes, "After 1950 the confluence of two major social and economic trends radically transformed the city [one racial, the other age]."[55] This shift impacted public education and future employees, which signaled a change in city economics. As white flight drained the city of school-age children, it also diminished city resources. Soon, the businesses followed the white workforce and slowly abandoned the city in tandem with the shift in industrial technology that needed a skilled workforce. Orr documented 1,811 manufacturing employers in 1951; this had dropped to 844 forty years later. The departure from the city was not solely along racial lines but heightened by the lack of improvements as a port city. Baltimore's deteriorating port and slow crawl to implement modern shipping technology made Newport News and Norfolk, Virginia, attractive and better-equipped options. Orr notes that "manufacturing jobs were replaced by advanced corporate and service sector jobs," which required a college education. This change, coupled with historical barriers, irreversibly hurt low-skilled and undereducated workers. Schools were the "last best hope" to avoid creating a perpetual poverty class. If the city could provide an adequate education of both soft and hard skills for the "neediest young people," this would empower them to become productive, employed Baltimore residents.

The shifting racial and economic demographics were most visible in the school system. When white administrators and teachers left the city for the surrounding counties, African American administrators and teachers gradually moved into positions and provided the best instruction for their students. Unfortunately, the lack of opportunities outside the classroom threatened to undermine efforts to stave off the crime that wooed them from the benefits of delayed gratification. Other students were pressured through peers or attempting to meet family needs that strained their human resources and developing minds. The classroom struggle in the midst of social changes had internal strife with the political bosses that influenced appointments and resources because public education is a governmental responsibility. Orr noted that only three Maryland governors from 1920 to 1960 were not from Baltimore city: Spiro Agnew in 1966, Harry Hughes in 1978 and 1982 and Parris Glendening in 1994. During that period (1920 to 1960), Baltimore held 49.3 percent of Maryland's population, augmenting the strength of political bosses. As the population shifted, the strength of political bosses weakened. However, the Democratic Party's stronghold within the city's electorate remained a deciding force within Maryland elections. Baltimore operated a system of patronage that at times transcended race and ethnic differences. The personal pursuit of a patron and recipient undercut broader issues and benefits where whole groups could benefit, especially within the African American community.

On the cusp of increasing needs and waning resources, Victorine realized that being on the City Council would provide leverage through public-private partnerships to supplement fickle government funding, as well as insulate the African American educational community and other demographics with alternative resources. In the midst of all the local and national turmoil, Baltimore appointed its first African American superintendent of schools, Robert N. Patterson, in 1970. Patterson, infused by the organizations among African American politicians, formed alliances with whites and African Americans to force the agenda of school funding while criticizing "political control" from outside the school system. Orr stated, "Patterson's reforms went against the grain," and he encountered resistance from within the African American community and city government that maintained the system of patronage.

Another influence in Victorine's decision to run for City Council might have been religious. An ardent Catholic, Victorine infused her life's mission with Christian-inspired duty. Many of the principles espoused by the CWDCC, Woman Power and other organizational affiliations openly embraced Christian principles. In January 1963, Cardinal Lawrence Shehan testified before the Baltimore City Council in favor of the Open Housing Bill. The bill failed, and Cardinal Shehan received death threats. In March, Shehan banned racial discrimination in the institutions of the Archdiocese of Baltimore, including schools, churches, social organizations and charitable institutions. To involve the laity, Shehan formed the first Archdiocesan Urban Commission in Baltimore to address the needs of Baltimoreans in the wake of drug- and poverty-inspired violence. Shehan penned a pastoral letter on racial justice. He demanded an end to racial discrimination institutionally and individually for the church and for society. Inspired by Dr. King and the mandate of Christ, Shehan exposed the Catholic Church's sin of bigotry and pleaded with all Catholics to uproot their narrow-mindedness. Shehan's public statement challenged all Baltimore Catholics to rise above the fray.

Victorine participated in the Archdiocesan Urban Commission, expanding her civic involvement to her beloved Catholic community. Much of the strife within the Catholic Church involved racial and ethnic differences that mirrored the neighborhoods throughout the city.

Above: Bishop William Boarders, Victorine and Councilwoman Barbara Mikulski. Campaign brochure. *Victorine Quille Adams papers, Box 12-14, folder 12. Courtesy of the Beulah M. Davis Special Collections, Morgan State University.*

Left: Victorine campaigning with a booster at Mondawmin Mall in 1975. Photographer A.R. Snowden. *Victorine Quille Adams papers, Box 12-14, folder 9. Courtesy of the Beulah M. Davis Special Collections, Morgan State University.*

Left to right: Senator Verda Welcome and Councilmembers Emma Michael, Victorine and Henry Parks. *Victorine Quille Adams papers, Box 12-14, folder 9. Courtesy of the Beulah M. Davis Special Collections, Morgan State University.*

Victorine's campaign truck. Campaign brochure. *Victorine Quille Adams papers, Box 12-14, folder 21. Courtesy of the Beulah M. Davis Special Collections, Morgan State University.*

It was during this turbulent decade that Victorine tossed her hat into the ring and moved from political educator to viable candidate. Three women had served on the City Council, finishing out terms left by their husbands' vacancies. The first woman elected to Baltimore City Council was Ella Bailey in 1937. Bailey represented the Sixth District and was unanimously elected. If elected, Victorine would be the first African American woman elected to the council. As a council member, she could craft policy and ensure beneficial laws were enacted on behalf of African Americans and marginalized residents.

STATE DELEGATE AND MADAME COUNCILWOMAN

The history of African Americans in the Maryland House of Delegates began in the wake of *Brown v. Board of Education*. The first African American delegate elected was Truly Hatchett in 1954. Hatchett ran as an independent candidate from the Fourth District. His victory bruised the Jack Pollack political machine. A native-born Baltimorean, Hatchett was over seventy years old when he was elected and served one term. Prior to his political career, Hatchett was a real estate dealer and insurance broker. He was the exalted ruler of the Monumental Elks Lodge of Baltimore and connected to the community through his activities with the YMCA. He served as chairman of the board of directors for the Druid Hill Avenue branch of the YMCA. He encouraged young men to run for office, sharing his experience. Winning was possible, he believed, in spite of an array of organized interests against them. Hatchett served along with another African American, Emory Cole.

Emory Cole was the only African American Republican to win the Fourth District. His first election was won by a margin of ninety-one votes when he unseated Democrat Milton Saul Jr. Cole entered politics after a thirty-year career in the postal system as a clerk at night and maintaining his law practice during the day. He could not run for office while employed with the postal system. As a Republican, he ran unopposed during the primary election. In an *Afro* article, Cole attributed his success as a direct result of being unknown, with "few friends to help and no enemies" to undermine his efforts. A Maryland native from Cockeysville, he was a graduate of Maryland State Teachers College and Howard University's Law School. He served in World War I. In 1923, he opened his law firm in Baltimore.

Victorine was the third of four trailblazing African American women to serve in the House of Delegates. The first was Verda Welcome, who grew into Maryland leadership through the rank and file work from community, organizational and sorority activities. She served for nine years in the Northwest Improvement Association (NIA). During her tenure, she elevated the NIA's visibility within the city. Through finding solutions to basic needs, from trash collection to health and welfare matters, life improved for residents. In 1957, as the national struggle for civil rights became a part of the nightly news programs, Verda felt compelled to seek a larger role within the political system of Maryland. Her sorority, Delta Sigma Theta, along with NCNW, Morgan students and others, pressed forward for greater inclusion in political affairs and decisions that impacted their lives. The efforts with her neighborhood association were limited to the city and specific area, but a political position within the Maryland government would have greater reach and a stronger influence. She decided to run for office and become a policy maker. After consulting with her husband, she entered the 1959 Maryland race for the state delegate position from the Fourth District of Baltimore city.

To win, she had to find a way to attract white votes. She reached out to white women who were concerned about gender equity. Race and gender matters plagued African American women; however, she understood that her voice would include equity for all marginalized people—but she needed to be elected first. Through her persuasive and passionate concern for marginalized voices, she attracted a number of white women. Racial tensions tugged at the seams of Baltimore, strengthened by class, ethnic and regional differences. She reasoned that if common ground could be reached, life would improve for all residents. In 1959, she won a seat in the Maryland House of Delegates, Fourth District. During her tenure from 1959 to 1961, she pushed for civil rights reform, equal protection under the law and social/humanitarian issues such as improved access for blind citizens and interracial marriage laws.

The positive impact her legislative successes brought enticed her to seek a larger position in Maryland politics. In 1962, she challenged Jack Pollack in a campaign for the State Senate. Her interracial and gendered appeal increased her popularity. Moreover, her legislative issues enriched all Marylanders and stood apart from the "old boys" network. The shifting climate in America emboldened her to strike out and use her personal being as more than a candidate but a voice of reason. In 1962, she won, becoming the first African American woman in the nation to be elected state senator. She served from the state of Maryland from 1962 to 1982.

Verda Welcome (*seated*); Victorine is standing to her left, and Henry Parks is standing. Verda Welcome collection, framed prints. *Courtesy of the Beulah M. Davis Special Collections, Morgan State University.*

The second woman was Irma George Dixon. Dixon was a Baltimorean educated at Coppin and Morgan who taught in Baltimore public schools. She, too, was a member of NCNW, the School Marms and Urban League. She served from 1959 to 1965 as a Democrat. She sponsored legislation that aided high school dropouts and female workers. Upon her untimely death in 1965 from cancer, an obituary in the *Afro* remarked that "education for her was higher ground" to be used for the greater good.

Victorine ran unsuccessfully in 1962 for the State Senate. In 1966, she successfully ran for the House of Delegates. But she resigned after a year and won election to the City Council. The turmoil of the nation impacted life in Baltimore. The white flight of the 1950s resulted in schools turning majority African American. At the same time, highway expansion exacerbated white flight along with middle-class flight, leaving entrenched poverty to gobble up additional lives and neighborhoods. As resourced

Senator and Minister Adam Clayton Powell, Senator Verda Welcome and Sterling Paige.
*Victorine Quille Adams papers, Box 12-15, folder 10. Courtesy of the Beulah M. Davis Special
Collections, Morgan State University.*

people left the city, politicians shifted their attention to issues that affected their demographic, leaving the urban center with a gradually waning voice in legislative affairs on the local level. Victorine's heart was in Baltimore. She loved the city, the people and its potential. She could not abandon it for the halls of the Maryland House of Delegates. When the opportunity to fill a position on the City Council arose, Victorine took it.

The fourth African American woman to serve in the House of Delegates was Lena K. Lee, an educator, attorney and politician. She was one of the earliest African American women elected to the Maryland General Assembly. Born in Sumter County, Alabama, she arrived in Baltimore in 1931. She earned a bachelor's degree from Morgan and a master's degree from New York University. In 1951, she earned her law degree from University of Maryland School of Law. While attending law school, she was principal of Henry H. Garnet Elementary School from 1947 until she retired in 1964. Similar to others, the civil rights movement appealed to her sense of duty, and that is when she considered running for a position in the House of Delegates. Elected in 1967, she won a seat in the Fourth District. During her tenure, she was very active in supporting civil rights legislation through fighting poorly constructed laws that were narrow or backward thinking. She sought to defeat them before they came to be placed on statewide ballots for citizens to vote.

All four women were educators and knew the conditions of the classrooms for both students and teachers were influenced by legislation crafted by the House of Delegates. Being in that strategic location informed from their years of service in the classroom, and embodied in black female bodies, they knew nuanced aspects of what laws would loosen or constrict economics, education and access for African Americans in general and women in particular. The foundation for good citizenship was an adequate education that empowered youth to view themselves and their future as contributing to the welfare of the state. When people are disconnected or made to feel unwanted, everyone loses. The city was a barometer that gauged the temperature of the nation, and Baltimore was running a high fever. Other cities opted to regulate conditions by increasing police officers and criminalizing poverty, but these measures did not help. Victorine and her colleagues knew that education, equity and understanding would readjust the urban temperature, allowing cooler heads to prevail and all residents an opportunity to explore their potential. In view of the crisis and trend of urban poverty, Baltimore needed Victorine's voice, resources and attention. In 1967, she resigned from the House Delegates to serve on Baltimore City Council, becoming the first African American woman candidate elected to serve.

The frustration of racism and poverty spread throughout the African American community of Baltimore. The gradual depletion of steady incomes, the Vietnam crisis, the increase in drug usage and the rhetoric of Black Power tugged at the threads of reason that connected the average person to calm and reason. Concurrently, a surge in black elected officials across the country sought to galvanize their power through collaboration with one another, civil rights organizations, religious institutions and white liberals to provide legislative and practical remedies to deteriorating conditions in urban areas. Victorine witnessed the decline in the quality of life for working-class people in Baltimore, while she also listened to suggestions from other elected officials on policy measures and partnerships that needed to be implemented. In her collection is a series of speech transcripts from notable men speaking on the social conditions in black urban neighborhoods.

In 1967, Percy E. Sutton helped organize the National Council of Black Elected Officials. This organization would provide a shared space where elected officials could collaborate, share and mentor one another. Sutton delivered the keynote address at the gathering, held at the University of Chicago. In September 1967, the interracial gathering met for three days in "mutual exploration, mutual exchange and collective learning" as individuals representing a variety of political, social and ideological differences in search of tools to remedy deteriorating urban conditions. Sutton remarked that louder voices were offering shortsighted and volatile solutions, while bickering among elected officials ignored the larger issue of neglect and needs desired by the black community. Sutton stated, "As elected officials we, each of us, must learn to better use this inherent [power and potential to move things] if we are to bring about meaningful change."[56] The black voter would not be placated by yesterday's tactics or political tokenism from the single black politician. These officials had to serve all of their constituents. Sutton concluded, "In this year of uprisings, rebellions and disorders, there were historical acts of heroism and struggle and of striking out at the chains of suppression and the conditions of unemployment, underemployment, under-education and deplorable housing."[57]

An address delivered by Lerone Bennett Jr. of the Johnson Publishing Company titled "The Politics of the Outsider: The Black Man's Role in American Politics" contrasted the "old" politics with the need for a "new" political strategy:

Somebody on the inside said once that politics is the art of the possible. But for the black outsider in America, politics in America has been the art of the impossible. It has been impossible, because it has been the art of trying to make a fundamental change in a political system by using the structures and instruments that were designed to perpetuate that system. It has been the art of the impossible because it has been the art of trying to make a social revolution with moderate tools that were invented to prevent social revolutions. It has been the art of the impossible because of the nature of politics, which is the art of making things impossible for outsiders, and because of the extremity of the black man's situation, which cannot be changed unless all things are made possible.[58]

Bennett crafts a portrait of African American history where using existing means brought some change and improvement; however, the turbulent times of nearly one hundred years of participation would require a radical solution to alleviate the burden black urban dwellers and all black people endured in America. He queried, "[Will it ever] be possible to achieve fundamental social and economic change by the practice of politics as defined by the insiders?" The uprisings from Watts to Detroit to Newark and Baltimore were rebellions against the old politics and structures that hoarded wealth, resources, decent housing and opportunity. Bennett's appeal to the elected officials and larger African American community was a need to reeducate oneself regarding African American history and stewardship. Their constituents were more than voters; they were African Americans and thus "kin" whose survival or failure would secure or destabilize not only the race but society as well. The African American voter needed to engage the process and understand the interconnectedness of policy, resources and representation. Many blacks did not believe they could effect change and were apathetic, while some politicians were not familiar with the sufferings of the urban working class and poor people. In closing, Bennett implored the attendees:

The relevant black politician must carry off the difficult fact of blending the traditional political skills with the skills of a reformer....Black officeholders [need] to use the whole range of parliamentary weapons in a nonviolent campaign <u>within</u> the political process. This would be a service not only to black Americans but to white Americans. For black people embody the most advanced social and economic interest of this society.... The mission of the black politician is to do what white politicians have *failed to do, define and actualize liberty and equality as a faith and a way of life. In the final analysis, Emmett John Hughes pointed out, the art of politics is "the subtle and sensitive attuning and disciplining of all words and deeds—not to mend the petty conflicts of the moment, nor to close some tiny gap in the discourse of the day—but to define and to advance designs and policies for a thousand tomorrows." And that is the historic mission of the black politician today: the advancing designs and policies for a thousand tomorrows for blacks and whites.*[59]

The commentary of Sutton and Bennett resonated with Victorine. She had, in fact, been a living embodiment of these practices and principles. Through her organizations, she employed the concept of voter education and accountability to those whose hands rocked cradles and counseled husbands, siblings, church members and all other social contacts. Similar to enlarging her classroom from schoolhouse to voter education sessions at the Charm Center, Baltimore city would be her classroom and all residents her pupils. Her decades of activism and husband were widely known. However, the fickle wind of people and politics would blow gently at other times. Those were calm moments; she, too, would experience harsh winds that raged against her because of her husband. Undaunted, Victorine kept her lines separate as much as possible yet favored her social consciousness through businesses affiliated with or directly related to her husband. Overall, her tenure as a councilwoman improved the lives of working-class and poor Baltimoreans.

Elected in 1967, she arrived at the tail end of Mayor Theodore R. McKeldin's second term in office. She would serve with two mayors: Thomas J. D'Alesandro III (1967–71) and William Donald Schaefer (1971–87). The first African American to serve as mayor was former councilman Clarence H. Burns. Burns, then president of the City Council, was selected to fill the remaining term for Schaefer, who ran and was elected governor of Maryland in 1987. In the 1987 election, Burns campaigned for mayor but lost in the Democratic primary to Kurt Schmoke. The *New York Times* reported that Burns rose to the heights of city leadership through the ranks. Born in 1918, he was an east-side Baltimorean educated in segregated schools. Most of his childhood and young adulthood was spent in efforts to earn money. He sold newspapers and vegetables and served in the army during World War II. His affable and dedicated nature earned him the moniker "Du" because he got things done. He served as a precinct worker for Mayor D'Alesandro. His first municipal job was locker room attendant

Victorine campaigning at a social event, May 25, 1975, at campaign headquarters in Mondawmin Mall. Photographer A.R. Snowden. *Victorine Quille Adams papers, Box 12-14, folder 9. Courtesy of the Beulah M. Davis Special Collections, Morgan State University.*

at a high school. In 1971, he won his first City Council seat. Through the 1970s and 1980s, Burns grew in influence on the City Council. He was the first African American president of the council. Although he was popular and influential, he failed to garner the support of African American political influencers to secure the vote for mayor. The first elected African American

William Donald Schaefer and Clarence "Du" Burns, both former Baltimore mayors. *Victorine Quille Adams papers, Box 12-14, folder 2. Courtesy of the Beulah M. Davis Special Collections, Morgan State University.*

mayor of Baltimore was Kurt Schmoke. His Yale, Oxford and Harvard University academic pedigree set Schmoke apart from Burns. Moreover, his youth and articulation served as a high benchmark for some African American residents who sought to overcome the increasing negativity white flight and poverty had rendered on Baltimore. Elected to a second term by 70 percent of the voters, Schmoke's administration attempted to address the crisis in urban living, from un/underemployment to implementing a needle exchange program. Both native sons, Burns and Schmoke left their marks in Baltimore's city administration with the intention of improving conditions and offering access to services to all residents.

Victorine served on a council with eighteen others representing six districts. She served under Schaefer and Walter S. Orlinsky when they were City Council presidents. Orlinsky was a career politician who served in the House of Delegates and led a failed campaign for Maryland governor. The members of the council during Victorine's tenure did not change much. Many ran and were reelected for more than two terms. Victorine served with Henry Parks during her first term and Barbara Ann

Mikulski during her second term. Mikulski started her career as a social worker and community organizer. A native of East Baltimore, Mikulski related to people and sought to bring about amicable solutions to social ills and problems. Elected to the council after delivering an impassioned speech praising ethnic America, she embraced her immigrant ancestry and working-class roots. Concerned, aware and desirous of providing opportunity, Mikulski morphed into a career politician who benefited her constituency. Her integrity and care resulted in her being the longest-serving woman in the history of the United States Congress and longest-serving senator in Maryland. Two other people of interest during Victorine's tenure were the father-and-son team of Emerson R. Julian and Emerson R. Julian Jr. The elder Dr. Julian, a physician, hailed from Victorine's Fourth District and was ideologically opposite of her and Michael B. Mitchell.

The *Afro* reported that Julian was dubbed a "maverick," "Crazy Horse" and "Uncle Tom," known for being outspoken. He openly spoke out on issues that bothered his conscience, regardless of where it placed him and even if it was on the wrong side of prevailing wisdom. Julian served under D'Alesandro and Schaefer. In those times fraught with racial tensions, Julian deplored the idea of appointing a black superintendent of schools. He disliked anti-poverty programs because he believed they enriched the administrators, offering crumbs to the needy people who needed more than Band-Aid solutions. The *Baltimore Sun* reported Orlinsky's statement after Julian's death that "Doc wasn't shy about being black but didn't necessarily play the traditional black games. He brought perspective to the Council." In 1978, he died from a heart attack. Julian's son decided to run for his father's seat on the council and was elected in 1978. Within several months, he relinquished his seat. The details of his decision are wrapped up in "Fourth district political maneuverings," according to the *Sun*. Julian swiped at Senator Verda Welcome as the "cause" for his decision. The *Sun* reported Julian saying, "Senator Welcome put her finger up in the air and sees which way the wind is going to go and then says, 'That's the way I'm going.'" Initially, he desired to continue his father's brand of open thinking as a living testament to his legacy. After the political rankling, he opted to continue the family tradition in medicine instead. Julian's uncle was Dr. Percy L. Julian, a noted chemist, researcher and civil rights activist. Uncle Percy held over 130 patents and innovated medication to treat glaucoma. So the ache of being displaced from the City Council did not stymie the career potential of Emerson R. Julian Jr.

EMMA M. MICHAEL

Emma M. Michael, housewife and community leader; educated in the public schools and Glassboro State College in New Jersey. Married to Charles F. Michael, vice-principal of Forest Park High School; mother of one daughter, Michele, a June graduate of Morgan State College.

Present member and former member of: Equal Opportunity Commission, 1962–65; Baltimore Community Relations Commission, 1965–68; Maryland Commission for the New York World's Fair, 1964–65; Administrative Committee Christian Social Relations of the Council of Churches; Board of Directors Crownsville State Hospital Auxiliary; Citizens' Advisory Committee to the Board of Education; Chairman sub-committee investigating juvenile detention institutions of the Baltimore Grand Jury; Baltimore City Police Community Relations Committee of the Northwestern District; Chairman, Legislative Committee of the Maryland League of Women's Clubs; Braddish Avenue Neighborhood Club.

She and her family attend Madison Avenue Presbyterian Church.

VICTORINE Q. ADAMS

Victorine Q. Adams, Baltimore born, Coppin College; B.S. degree, Morgan State College, graduate work New York University School of Business. She is married to businessman William L. Adams; has one stepdaughter, and a granddaughter. She is an active member of St. Peter Claver Church.

Former teacher, business woman, civic leader. Pioneer in the register-to-vote drives in Baltimore; organized Democratic Women, Woman Power, Inc.; awarded Afro Honor Roll plaque in 1948 for interesting women to work in politics; Director of 1964 Register-to-Vote National Campaign; Director of "get-out-the-vote" for Johnson in 1964; member National Sorority Phi Delta Kappa, Sigma Gamma Rho; NAACP; YWCA; Mental Hygiene Society; 4th Dist. Democratic Org.; Business & Professional Club; Health and Welfare Council of Baltimore area; Board of Trustees, Provident Hospital and Advance Savings & Loan Asso.; National Council of Negro Women, organizing the first associate membership in Baltimore; United Women's Democratic Club of Maryland; campaign coordinator for the Democratic Party in Baltimore; Member of House of Delegates from the Fourth District.

HENRY G. PARKS, JR.

Henry G. Parks, civic leader, public servant, businessmen; graduate of Ohio State University, College of Commerce; graduate work in marketing; father (2 daughters), grandfather (2 grand-children).

City Council incumbent; President, Parks Sausage Co., an employer in Baltimore City; member Chamber of Commerce Baltimore, Inc.; Chamber of Commerce of the United States; life member NAACP; Provident Hospital Board; Urban League National Board; Advertising Club of Baltimore; Maryland Judicial Selection Council, Inc.; National Advisory Council, Small Business Administration-Md.; Board of Directors, National Interracial Council for Business Opportunity; Voluntary Council on Equal Opportunity, Inc.; Regional Planning Council; prime mover for OIC in Baltimore, model demonstration cities project, helping neighborhood groups solve area problems, totally interested in jobs for the unemployed and underemployed.

Campaign brochure. Victorine Quille Adams papers, Box 12-14, folder 2. Courtesy of the Beulah M. Davis Special Collections, Morgan State University.

During her tenure, Victorine introduced a number of bills and resolutions. She introduced resolutions on behalf of notable living and deceased people both local and national, such as Paul Robeson, athlete, actor and civil rights activist; Dr. Robert J. Hill, podiatrist, Prince Hall Mason and community organizer; William A. Stanford, professor at Coppin State and churchman; and Stephanie B. McManus, first African American to be the Naval Academy's official color girl. The color girl is an element of a ceremony beginning in 1871 when the brigade flag is transferred from the outgoing color company to the midshipman appointed as the incoming commander of the new color company. McManus was an Annapolis native and graduate of Fisk University who desired a career in law. Victorine expressed congratulations to McManus in breaking the "color barrier" in the Naval Academy.

Council president Orlinsky and the council passed a resolution on the occasion of the death of Victorine's father, Joseph C. Quille. The resolution read:

Joseph C. Quille a native Baltimorean and father of two children, who made substantial contributions to the business and political life of Baltimore City, departed this life on January 15, 1976. A mass of the resurrection was held for him at St. Peter Claver Church.

Mr. Quille offered to his children and to the community a model of a man who worked hard in order to give his children the priceless possession of a good education.

He was for many years a bartender and an excellent one and he served at the famed hotels Rennert and Caswell. He later served as the manager of Little Willie's Inn and Little Joe's Inn in northwest Baltimore.

He was also one of the first black chauffeurs in Baltimore City and one of the organizers of the Chauffeurs Club. He was also an organizer of the Pleasure Strutters Club, a well-known social club of his day.

Mr. Quille possessed a fine singing voice. An accomplished piano player by ear, he played gratuitously for many affairs given by his friends.

He was a kind and affectionate person and known by many hundreds of people as "Daddy Joe." He attended and was a member of St. Peter Claver Church.

Mr. Quille leaves to his children, William C. Quille and Councilwoman Victorine Adams, a fine legacy—work hard and faithfully and always bear in mind the plight of your fellow man; be it, therefore

Resolved by the City Council of Baltimore, That in the death of Joseph C. Quille the city has lost a fine and upright citizen who contributed to the well-being of its people and his loss will be mourned by the many Baltimoreans who knew him.[60]

Victorine also introduced bills that worked to improve life for working-class and poor people in Baltimore. In February 1976, she proposed a resolution, Bill No. 149, requesting the State Social Services Administration to maintain its contribution to the Emergency Service Center. The increasing needs of the public losing their employment strained the resources available through the Emergency Service Center. This need was exacerbated by the possibility of the General Public Assistance Emergency Program shutting its doors. She suggested that Maryland, through the State Social Services Administration, be allowed to request it keep its current funding level. This bill was referred to the Budget and Finance Committee. The loss of semi-skilled employment plagued residents and led to additional resolutions requesting financial assistance from the state government.

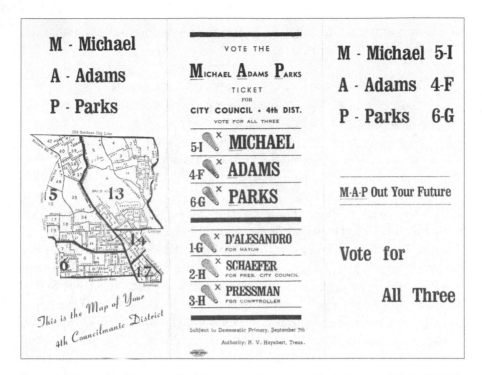

Campaign brochure. *Victorine Quille Adams papers, Box 12-14, folder 2. Courtesy of the Beulah M. Davis Special Collections, Morgan State University.*

In March 1976, she proposed a resolution, Bill No.158, requesting the board of estimates to maintain the General Public Assistance Emergency Program in its budget. There was discussion in the board of estimates to remove the budgetary appropriation for 1,500 unemployables. These people, Victorine asserted, were not criminals or drug users; they were law-abiding citizens who did not possess particular skills that could transfer into this day of economic depression. These people were under the age of thirty and needed the funds to maintain a standard of living while seeking employment that suited their capacity. If the appropriation was removed, it would lead to criminal activity in an attempt to survive. Victorine included the fact that this bill supported Senate Bill 737, which placed the fiscal responsibility on the State of Maryland, not Baltimore. The bill was amended and adopted.

In June 1976, Bill No. 394 requested that President Gerald R. Ford reconsider his reduction in the food stamp program. The Ford administration proposed to reduce the Food Stamp Program by $1.2 billion. The budget did not see the human factor involved in the devastating fiscal choice. That cut would stop aid to 5.3 million people and greatly reduce aid to another 5.5 million people. Victorine stated:

> *Maryland and 25 other states together with a great number of labor unions, church groups, and Mayor Schaefer, representing the Conference of Mayors, have filed suit to block the Ford Administration's proposed revisions. The plaintiffs have filed more than 800 pages of legal briefs and affidavits in the suit and they hope to obtain a temporary restraining order in order that the food stamp benefits may continue.*[61]

This bill was adopted. However, the nation was transitioning from Republican Ford to Democrat Jimmy Carter. Both administrations believed that the Food Stamp Program needed reform. Ford desired to reduce the bureaucracy and give the state and local government more control through block grants. Ford proposed legislation twice to reform the Food Stamp Program, but it was stalled in Congress and directed by the Department of Agriculture. During the transition, the food stamp chapter of proposed changes was designed to "tighten eligibility standards" for the program, which would increase those disqualified based on income, not cost of living. To combat the lack, Victorine approached churches, philanthropists and corporate charities to contribute and/or provide for the poorest residents.

The fight for aid was not the only entanglement Victorine endured. In 1975 and again in 1979, Victorine tangled with longtime social friend and political colleague Verda Welcome. In August 1975, the *Sun* reported that "factional war" was brewing among Democrats in West Baltimore. Welcome threatened to urge her organization to withdraw its endorsement of Victorine's reelection, in part from Western W. Ivey, who withdrew his bid for City Council for the opening on the Democratic State Central Committee in the Fortieth Legislative District. The seat became available when Dr. Henry C. Welcome, Senator Welcome's husband, passed away in July, leaving a space on the three-person committee. She ran to fill his seat and lost. The state central committees were empowered to fill vacancy in the General Assembly. The maneuverings through "traditionally byzantine politics" in the Fourth District resulted in Ivey's redirected focus to the Democratic State Central Committee. Senator Welcome's last-minute bid, nominated by Howard P. Rawlings, disturbed the delicate power shift for Ivey. Another fly in the ointment was Ivey's attempt a year earlier to unseat Senator Welcome. This enraged Welcome's supporters, in part because of Ivey's support coming from the

Metro Democratic Organization, founded by Willie Adams. Welcome's displeasure was justified; however, Willie Adams had funded her earlier efforts to state leadership and was snubbed by Welcome, who sought to distance herself from his unsavory activities. If Ivey won, then the Fortieth District Central Committee would be filled with Willie Adams's Metro Democratic–minded people. The *Sun* reported that Welcome "fought like a gladiator" in an effort to win. The nine-year feud between the Metro Democratic Organization and Welcome's Fourth District Democratic Organization resulted in direct attacks against Willie Adams and his Metro Democratic Organization.

In August 1979, Frank Conway of the Metro Democratic Organization demanded Welcome step down as state senator. Conway asserted that Welcome's open attack against Victorine was toxic. Conway also coveted Welcome's Senate seat. The vitriol flew between the two Democratic organizations. Welcome was called a liar and Adams dubbed a manipulator. The ugliness stemmed from failed unity talks between the two political brokers from the Fourth District. Willie reassured voters that Victorine was a viable candidate with or without an endorsement from Welcome. The *Sun* reported that the flap between Welcome and Victorine stemmed from a rejected $5,000 printing cost for Welcome's campaign materials possibly from Willie's charitable contributions. Victorine won her reelection bid in 1979. The damage to the social friendship found space in local newspapers; however, the progress for social justice moved along, and both women left an indelible mark on city and state legislation, improving the quality and opportunities for all citizens. In a December 1996 article in the *Sun* that recounted the fifty years of the CWDCC, Victorine stated, "We worked together till it got to the point where we could disagree." Such was a bittersweet result of organizing the vote in Baltimore.

Also in 1979, Councilman Julian sponsored a zoning ordinance allowing for construction of a fast-food eatery in Mondawmin Mall. The residents near the mall did not want the eatery in their neighborhood. Victorine did not oppose the zoning ordinance. Moreover, the eatery was being proposed by a company in which Willie held a financial interest. To uproot Victorine, Welcome backed Michael Mitchell and supported Mary Adams (no relation to Victorine). The *Sun* picked up the story, noting that the poorer sections of Baltimore did not need another fast-food eatery. The zoning ordinance was withdrawn as a result of public pressure. The *Sun* went further to denounce Victorine as "not developed" but a representative of Willie and "his political cronies," sacrificing the larger needs of the Fourth District. In concert with

Welcome, the *Sun* wrote, "[Victorine] should be rejected by the voters," allowing Mitchell, the more qualified candidate. Mitchell hailed from a prominent Baltimore family. His father, Clarence Mitchell Jr., was the director of the Washington, D.C. NAACP. His mother, famed lawyer and activist Juanita Jackson Mitchell, was no stranger to Victorine. She ran again and was elected, and Mitchell, too, was elected in 1975 at the age of twenty-nine to the City Council. The animus between Victorine and Verda simmered throughout the remaining years of their lives. The differences were more veiled than overt, and the two women ended up endorsing Agnes Welch to replace Victorine, but only when she had decided against another term in office.

In the 1980s, Victorine joined other council members and proposed Bill No. 1367. This resolution sought positive assistance for the unemployed. Many corporations that enlarged the worker rolls in Baltimore trickled out of the city. Future mayor Schmoke noted that Johns Hopkins replaced Bethlehem Steel, and the workforce needed to improve their skills for the budding technological industry. For those workers unable to improve their skills, the positive assistance for the unemployed would create a collaboration between a newly formed public-private committee tasked with generating ideas to find employable opportunities for the newly unemployed worker. The bill noted, "Those stricken with unemployment lack the knowledge or facilities for coping with the accompanying problems, and are unaware that in many cases interim solutions exist."[62] Therefore, a public-private partnership would locate spaces where solutions could be found to ameliorate unemployment and outdated job skills. The private institutions represented banking, real estate, retail, utility agencies and human resource groups. The committee would also offer life skills information, such as staving off foreclosure and locating medical services. This bill was assigned to the Urban Affairs Committee.

Victorine served on the City Council Task Force on Unemployment and the City Council Task Force on Homelessness. Impassioned and greatly concerned for the quality of life for working-class and poor residents, she advocated and innovated ways to bring attention and services to the neediest residents. She did so with dignity and research data to support the claims that an education, adequate employment, clean housing and viable opportunity elevated the quality for all Baltimoreans. Through the City Council, she did her best to level the playing field and articulate the needs of people who often looked like her but lacked opportunity and access, not capacity or ability. In recounting her tenure on the City Council, her proudest accomplishment was the Baltimore Fuel Fund. The Fuel Fund was a public-private partnership that raised money from charitable contributions, corporations and private individuals, all given to social services to dispense to families needing financial assistance with heating costs. There was no direct benefit to Victorine or Willie; however, his "money" continued to remain tainted in the eyes of many Baltimoreans. Nevertheless, Willie openly and privately contributed to numerous philanthropic endeavors, if not directly then vicariously through businesses he initially funded throughout Baltimore. The Fuel Fund embodied Victorine's zealous passion to provide and care for her fellow man. The idea, birthed by Victorine, was embraced by religious and business leaders. The fickle nature of politics required that the early Fuel Fund Committee locate a space to centralize the fund so that it would be self-perpetuating, without bureaucratic red tape.

Unfortunately, three years in the wake of her death, the Victorine Q. Adams Fuel Fund encountered funding challenges. The partnership between the Victorine Q. Adams Fuel Fund and the Fuel Fund of Maryland was at odds regarding how the funds were maintained. Charles

Victorine (*seated*) with a child next to Henry Parks with unidentified people. Campaign brochure. *Victorine Quille Adams papers, Box 12-14, folder 17. Courtesy of the Beulah M. Davis Special Collections, Morgan State University.*

Victorine in an advertisement for the Baltimore Fuel Fund campaign Paddle for People, a fund and awareness raiser. Campaign brochure. *Victorine Quille Adams papers, Box 12-14, folder 17. Courtesy of the Beulah M. Davis Special Collections, Morgan State University.*

W. Griffin, president of the VQA fund, alleged racial insensitivity, while Marnell Cooper of Maryland cited fiscal irresponsibility. Started in 1979, Victorine's Fuel Fund partnered private organizations and Baltimore Gas and Electric to fund a program to assist Baltimore's neediest families. George Coling of the National Fuel Funds Network revered Victorine as a pioneering hero. Unfortunately, the VQA fund overspent money, requiring the partnering BGE to pay upward of $248,395 in energy assistance in late 2007. A concession was made, resulting in Victorine's name being removed from the reconstructed Fuel Fund of Maryland. The contentious decision severed ties with Victorine's name and legacy. The current incarnation offers assistance with contributions from other groups such as the Salvation Army.

RETIRING FROM PUBLIC SERVICE

In July 1983, after serving four terms on the City Council, Victorine announced she would not seek another term. At age seventy-one, she ended her public service. She endorsed Agnes Welch, a community activist seeking public office, to replace her on the council. Agnes Welch was elected to the Baltimore City Council and served from 1983 to 2010. During her tenure, she served as the chair on Urban Affairs and Aging. Welch, twelve years Victorine's junior, also attended Morgan State College, was an educator and worked for social justice. She, too, was a Catholic and attended St. Edward's Roman Catholic Church. Welch retired at eighty-five yet remained a tireless advocate for the elderly and neediest residents of Baltimore.

Victorine prepared a statement to articulate her decision. The decision to retire resulted from a heartfelt conversation with her husband, Willie. It was ultimately her decision but measured against the insight of her husband of forty-eight years. The *Baltimore Sun* reported Victorine as saying, "This decision is a difficult one, because I loved my job." After a lifetime of organizing women, fighting political systems, participating in numerous organizations, running a business, lecturing around the region and mentoring young people, Victorine was justifiably tired. She explained that the physical act of politics, such as campaigning, was over. However, she would continue in a new role through less physical efforts, from philanthropy to hosting meetings through the CWDCC (now the Democratic Women's Committee). During her remarks, she voiced support for Donald Schaefer and Clarence H. "Du" Burns in their reelection efforts. She shared her post-council plans, including documenting and cataloging political memorabilia and papers collected over forty years.

In July 1983, writing about Victorine, the *Sun* reflected that her tenure on the City Council left a rich legacy of representing poor residents. She conscientiously addressed the problems of the underprivileged. Critics faulted her for not using her position to craft legislation to shift resources to specific areas. She employed the private sector to meet select needs or fund select programs. The fickle nature of politics and the ugly specter of discrimination along racial and class lines influenced her decision to ensure that special programs were consistently funded to meet the needs of her constituency.

Reminisce the Great Pioneer

In a program book celebrating the Fuel Fund, Delores and Abner Lee remarked that Victorine was a woman who had "foresight to recognize a problem, organizing talent, tenacity and humility." She did not crave attention but solutions to problems. During the dark days of intense segregation, she joined forces with Mary McLeod Bethune, an educator, along with other educators to teach African American women about the power of the franchise. Employing the same skills in her classroom instruction, empowerment and repetition, she galvanized hundreds of women through the CWDCC. She served as a member, not a potentate. She joined other organizations, sharing and learning, always growing. Her faith kept the goal in mind—not self-recognition or popularity but relevance through using her God-given talents to make the world a better place for all mankind.

This sense of selflessness is an aspect of Christian faith. Victorine's Catholic upbringing would expose her to the suffering Christ, as well as the biblical scriptures that indicate the greatest of you is the servant, as in Mark 10:45: "For even the Son of Man did not come to be served, but to serve, and to give His life—a ransom for many." This sense of contributing was an intrinsic aspect of her civic activity. Moreover, many African American club women opted to make similar endeavors to improve conditions within their respective locales infused with the similar biblical mandate of servanthood. Many of the rituals, oaths and pledges from sororities to civic groups used biblical allegory, and many of the women held positions within their churches. The fusion of faith and activism was seamless. The Christian life is one of stewardship. The believer is afforded a talent/skill that is to be used for the betterment of mankind. Victorine's intellectual ability, organizational skills and access to money afforded her the ability to enrich the lives of those around her. The conditions of African Americans, women and the poor were areas of need that she could improve through using her innate and material resources.

Two years after her death, in the spring of 2008, the Hanlon Park neighborhood welcomed the Victorine Q. Adams Community Garden. The garden, located on Carlisle Avenue and Vickers Road, "has sprouted into a charming flower and vegetable habitat for humanity."[63] Neighbors plant and reap vegetables. The surplus of the garden's harvest is donated to St. Cecilia's Soup Kitchen and Food Pantry. As of 2018, the community garden reported that some two hundred pounds of fresh vegetables have been donated. According to the community garden's website, the "[g]arden offers a place of solitude and an open grassy area for community gatherings as well as social events." Prior to being selected as the site for the Victorine Q. Adams Community Garden, the space was occupied by filth and sick animals. Since being sponsored by the Baltimore City Adopt-A-Lot program—accompanied by numerous commercial and private donations, among which was the William L. Adams Foundation—the lot is now home to "butterflies, honey bees, robins and squirrels."

The community garden is the meeting place for the Green Thumbers Garden Club. These avid urban farmers seek to prepare the land for planting and oversee the maintenance of the separate plots. The Green Thumbers operate as a co-op encouraging community engagement and fellowship. Another charitable aspect of the garden is teaching youth about gardening. They decided to make annual donations to St. Cecilia's, sharing their bounty with less fortunate people. Their aspirations reach beyond Baltimore, as discussions bubble up about participating in the Amish Markets in Pennsylvania. Miriam Avins, founder of Baltimore Green Space, wrote in the *Baltimore Sun* suggesting that the tax code for privately run parks versus city-funded parks impedes citizens from rehabilitating the empty lots throughout Baltimore. She believes the tax code needs to change to the benefit of the residents and planet. A modified code would "strengthen and protect" these natural spaces.

Thus, the lines of Victorine's life grew from her heart. She loved Baltimore and believed in compassion. Victorine knew the human lifeline was subject to seasonal changes. In the summer of her youth, she pursued an education. Challenging herself and thinking about making a difference, she taught elementary school students. In the autumn of her life, she deeply invested in social movements that appealed to her sense of justice during her adulthood. As issues demanded a greater voice, she joined organizations, founded the CWDCC, co-founded Woman Power, Incorporated and campaigned for public office, placing herself within the halls of power to craft legislation benefiting all Baltimoreans. In the winter of her life, when her strength waned, she stepped aside, offering another person an opportunity to craft compassionate legislation for all Baltimoreans. When she stepped from the halls of power to her private home, she continued to contribute through philanthropic means, offering scholarships, wisdom and support to rising generations. In springtime, Victorine blossomed anew in a posthumous form through the Victorine Q. Adams Fuel Fund and increasing the number of African American women in Baltimore politics, as well as the William L. and Victorine Q. Adams Foundation.

Left to right: Willie, Victorine, scholarship winner Raymond Mooring, Blanche Rodgers and Dr. Freeman Hrabowski. Mooring was awarded the Adams/Rodgers Scholar within the Meyerhoff Scholarship Program. The program supported high-achieving incoming freshmen who were committed to promoting minorities in careers of science, mathematics and engineering or computer science. December 16, 1995. Campaign brochure. *Victorine Quille Adams papers, Box 12-14, folder 22. Courtesy of the Beulah M. Davis Special Collections, Morgan State University.*

In essence, Victorine is a part of Baltimore's history, with a number of distinctions. She was the first African American woman elected to the City Council. She was the first woman to serve as acting president of the City Council when President Clarence "Du" Burns was traveling internationally. A lover of poetry, it was said at her funeral:

> *Reminisce the great pioneer—forever remember her*
> *Not with your head down and your back slump*
> *But with your head held high standing in the light of hope*
> *With a helping hand and a heart of courage and compassion*
> *With purposed lives of a greater scope*
> *Carving a fresh path of righteousness for the next generation*
> *Remember the pillar, the statue, the dreams—of a phenomenal woman*
> *In our spirits we'll always remember the legacy of the great Victorine.*[64]

Hope, a heart of courage, compassion and a helping hand—those words describe the spirit of Victorine's doing. They also embody her legacy to those who knew her and those who seek to know her through her archival collection, legislation and living memorials that remain in her hometown.

VICTORINE Q. ADAMS TIMELINE

April 28, 1912	Victorine Elizabeth Quille Adams was born in Baltimore to Joseph and Estelle Tate Quille.
1924?	Victorine graduated from Public School #104.
1928?	Victorine graduated from Frederick Douglass High School.
1930	Victorine graduated from Coppin Normal School.
July 28, 1935	Victorine married William "Little Willie" Adams.
June 1938	The Adams family home is bombed. In one article, Willie Adams stated that it was not numbers-related but an attempt to shake him down. He publicly accused Julius Fink. He alleged that Fink ordered him to "kick in" 5 percent of earnings from his successful tavern. The Adamses lived above the tavern they owned. The police suspected underworld threats from neighboring crime bosses in Philadelphia or New York. After testimony and an indictment, Fink was charged with assault with intent to kill. Victorine suffered nervous shock, while other residents in the building were badly bruised. No life was lost.

June 1940	Victorine graduated summa cum laude from Morgan State College with a BS in education.
1940s	Victorine taught in Baltimore public schools.
May 1942	Victorine participated in protesting discrimination, resulting in change. The Citizens Committee for Justice comprised 150 organizations that led a march on Annapolis, Maryland, demanding the governor address the concerns of African Americans. In response, Governor Herbert R. O'Connor created a commission of fourteen persons, of whom five were black. Regardless, they requested of the governor myriad items: to end discrimination in war industries in Maryland; to investigate police killings of unarmed black citizens and to appoint "colored" uniformed policemen; and to appoint a "colored" manager to the board of managers at Crownsville State Hospital, an asylum for mentally ill blacks.
1946	Victorine founded and organized the Colored Women's Democratic Campaign Committee.
1948	Victorine conducted a "Register to Vote" drive for Democratic women. She registered more than four thousand new voters in one month.
1948	Victorine worked as manager of the Charm Center, a women's clothing boutique.
1958	Victorine co-founded Woman Power, Incorporated, with Ethel P. Rich. Woman Power was a nonpartisan group of black women dedicated to political education, information, action and power.
1963	Victorine served as chairman of Provident Hospital Development Program and raised funds to operate the hospital.
1963–64	Victorine was director of a registration drive that put thirty thousand new voters on the books.
1964	Victorine was campaign director for U.S. President Lyndon B. Johnson and the Democratic slate.
1966	Victorine was elected to the Maryland House of Delegates, Fourth District.

1967	Victorine was elected to Baltimore City Council, Fourth District.
1970	Victorine was elected to the State Central Committee, Fourth District.
1978–79	Victorine founded the Baltimore Gas and Electric Company's Fuel Fund. This program was created to assist low-income families with their utility bills in the winter.
1983	Victorine retired after four terms on the City Council.
January 8, 2006	Victorine died from poorly differentiated adenocarcinoma of the left parotid gland. She is buried in Arbutus Memorial Park in Arbutus, Maryland.

VICTORINE Q. ADAMS'S MEMBERSHIPS

Altar Guild of St. Peter's Claver Church
Archdiocesan Urban Commission (member)
Baltimore City Council (acting president)
Barrett Training School for Colored Girls (board member)
Charmettes, Incorporated
Citizen of the Year, Omega Psi Phi, Pi Omega Chapter (1975)
City Council Task Force on the Homeless (member)
City Council Task Force on Unemployment (chairwoman)
Colored Women's Democratic Campaign Committee (founder)
Community Fund (volunteer)
Coppin State University (alumni association/advisory board)
Council for Cultural Progress
Fourth District Democratic Club
Girl Scouts of America (board member)
Hanlon Park Improvement Association
Health and Welfare Council Homeless Task Force
Iota Phi Lambda Sorority, Incorporated
League of Women Voters
Martiniques, Inc.
Morgan State College (alumni association)
National Association for the Advancement of Colored People

National Association of Negro Business and Professional Women's Clubs
National Council of Negro Women
National Democratic Convention, Atlantic City (delegate, 1964)
National Organization of Women
Pennsylvania Avenue Business Men's Association (vice president)
Phi Delta Kappa Sorority, Incorporated
Provident Hospital (Board of Trustees)
Red Cross (volunteer)
School Marms
Sigma Gamma Rho Sorority, Incorporated
United Women's Democratic Club
Women Power, Incorporated (co-founder)
Young Men's Christian Association (co-chairman/building fund)
Young Women's Christian Association (building fund drive)

NOTES

Preface

1. Doug Donovan, "Work of Adams Did Not Go Unnoticed," *Baltimore Sun*, January 14, 2006.
2. Kennedy, "Victorine Adams."
3. Ibid., 87.

Chapter 1

4. Roger Nissly, "He Parlays a Bucket and Rags into 17 Parking Garages," *Afro American*, August 13, 1966, 5.
5. Bettye M. Moss, "If You Ask Me," *Afro American*, September 20, 1969, 5.
6. St. Francis Xavier Catholic Church, "History."
7. Sister Reginald Gerdes, "St. Peter Claver."
8. Ibid.
9. Morrow, "Undoubtedly a Bad State of Affairs," 261.
10. Ibid., 261–62.
11. Ibid., 262.
12. Ibid., 265.
13. www.patheos.com/blogs/mcnamarasblog/2009/04/thomas-wyatt-turner-1877-1978.html.
14. McNamara, "Thomas Wyatt Turner."

15. Power, "Apartheid Baltimore Style," 289.
16. National Register of Historic Places Registration Form, Sandtown-Winchester Survey. African American School No. 9. Prepared by Elizabeth Jo Lampl and Kay Fanning/Architectural Historians. Survey No. B-4467. United States Department of the Interior National Park Service.
17. *Afro American*, February 1915.

Chapter 2

18. Vaz, "'We Intend to Run It,'" 89.
19. Cheshire, *They Call Me Little Willie*, 14.
20. Ibid., 20.
21. Ibid., 26.
22. Ibid., 27.
23. Ibid., 33.
24. Ibid., 255.
25. Ibid., 33.
26. Ibid.
27. Kahrl, "New Negroes at the Beach," 338.
28. Ibid., 346.
29. Fletcher, *Historically African American Leisure Destinations*, 3.

Chapter 3

30. The National Council of Negro Women, 1935–1949, NABWH 001_S05_B16_F263.
31. Remarks Made at the Dedicatory Services of the Building for the National Council of Negro Women, Inc., NABWH 001_S05_B10_F182.
32. Greater Baltimore Section, NCNW NABWH_001_SG1_04_correspondence. Mary McLeod Bethune Council House, NPS.
33. Ibid.
34. VQA Collection, Box 12-6, Folder 2.
35. Crenson, *Baltimore*, 396.
36. Ibid.
37. VQA Papers, Box 12-6, Folder 2.
38. Ibid.
39. Ibid.

40. Ibid.
41. Ibid.
42. Ibid.
43. Ibid.
44. Ibid.
45. Ibid.
46. Ibid.
47. Ibid.
48. Ibid., Box 12-1, Folder 3.

Chapter 4

49. *Morgan College Bulletin*, 30.
50. Ibid., 34.
51. VQA Papers, Box 12-4, Folder 1.
52. Adams, "Provident Hospital."
53. Ibid.
54. VQA Papers, Box 12-9, Folder 3.

Chapter 5

55. Orr, *Black Social Capital*, 64.
56. VQA speech, Box 12-11, Folder 18.
57. Ibid.
58. Ibid.
59. Ibid.
60. VQA Papers, Box 12-11, Folder 3.
61. Ibid.
62. Ibid.
63. 3200 Carlisle Block Association, "Victorine Q. Adams Community Garden."
64. VQA Papers, Box 12-1, Folder 1.

BIBLIOGRAPHY

Primary Sources

Victorine Quille Adams Papers. Beulah M. Davis Special Collections, Earl S. Richardson Library, Morgan State University, Baltimore, MD.

Preface

Kennedy, Kellian. "Victorine Adams: The Civil Rights and Social Justice Movement in Baltimore." Master's thesis, University of Maryland–Baltimore County, 2012.

Chapter 1

Afro American. "City Sixth in Size but Far Back in Civil Rights Law." July 22, 1950, 13.
———. "Education Still Plays Key Role in the Life of Ms. Kate Sheppard." October 25, 1975, 12.
———. "5 Names on Governor's Commission." May 23, 1942, 9.
———. "Prof. Mason Hawkins Speaks at Cheyney." April 17, 1915, 1.
———. "Summer School in First Week at Morgan." July 8, 1933, 10.
———. "We Won't Fight Unless, Hastie Tells Morgan." June 15, 1940, 6.

Baltimore's Civil Rights Heritage. "1930–1965." baltimoreheritage.github. io/civil-rights-heritage/overview/1930-1965.

Carteh, Michael. "Maryland's Gov. O'Connor Is Dignified, Friendly, Timid." *Afro American*, October 2, 1943, 2.

Garrett Jones, Lula. "Gadabout-ing in Baltimore." *Afro American*, August 11, 1934.

Maryland Inventory of Historic Properties. Sandtown-Winchester Survey, February 1992.

McNamara, Pat. "Thomas Wyatt Turner (1877–1978)." McNamara's Blog. www.patheos.com/blogs/mcnamarasblog/2009/04/thomas-wyatt-turner-1877-1978.html.

Morrow, Diane Batta. "Undoubtedly a Bad State of Affairs: The Oblate Sisters of Providence and the Josephite Fathers, 1877–1903." *Journal of African American History* 101, no. 3 (Summer 2016).

Moss, Bettye M. "If You Ask Me." *Afro American*, September 20, 1969, 5.

Neverdon-Morton, Cynthia. *Afro-American Women of the South and the Advancement of the Race, 1895–1925*. Knoxville: University of Tennessee, 1991.

Nissly, Roger. "He Parlays a Bucket and Rags into 17 Parking Garages." *Afro American*, August 13, 1966, 5.

Perkins, Linda M. "Heed Life's Demands: The Educational Philosophy of Fanny Jackson Coppin." *Journal of Negro Education* 51, no. 3 (n.d.): 181–90.

Power, Garrett. "Apartheid Baltimore Style: The Residential Segregation Ordinances of 1910–1913," *Maryland Law Review* 42, no. 2 (1982): 289.

Sister Reginald Gerdes. "St. Peter Claver Is 120 Years Strong." *Catholic Review*, January 19, 2012. www.archbalt.org/st-peter-claver-is-120-years-strong-2.

St. Francis Xavier Roman Catholic Church. "History." www.historicfrancisxavier.org/HISTORY.html.

U.S. History. "Maryland—The Catholic Experiment." www.ushistory.org/us/5a.asp.

Chapter 2

Afro American. "Agreement Reached in Golf Course Case: Provides for Colored Golfers to Use 3 City Parks Pending Improvements." May 1, 1943, 10.

———. "Baltimore Golf Links Open to All: Judge's Rule Climaxes 7-Year Legal Battle." June 26, 1948, 1.

———. "Calls Bomb Shakedown: White Suspect Held on Little Willie's Story BOMB MISSES HER." June 25, 1938, 24.

———. "City Fights Jury Decision Opening Golf Courses: Jury Finds Colored Facilities below Par: Baltimore Seeks to Nullify Action Opening All Links." July 4, 1942, 42.

———. "Maryland Court Reverses Order Opening Baltimore Golf Courses to All: Okeys Segregation, 'Impressed' by Suggestion Colored Citizens Should Get Along Without Golf." December 19, 1942.

Baltimore Sun. "Black Business, Politics Mixed—Often in Jewish Alliance." March 19, 1979, A8.

———. "Political Leader Lloyd Randolph Dies." October 23, 1983, B14.

———. "Rules Married Women Retain Right to Teach." June 4, 1924, 26.

Cheshire, Mark R. *They Call Me Little Willie: The Life Story of William L. Adams.* N.p.: Ellison's Books, 2016.

Dawkins, Marvin P., and Walter C. Farrell. "Joe Louis and the Struggle of African American Golfers for Visibility and Access." *Challenge* 14, no. 1, article 6.

Dorsey, Maurice W. *Businessman First: Remembering Henry G. Parks, Jr. 1916–1989: Capturing the Life of a Businessman Who Was African American.* N.p.: Xlibris, 2013.

Dresser, Michael. "Former Governor Marvin Mandel Dies." *Baltimore Sun,* August 31, 2015, Obituaries.

Fletcher, Patsy Mose. *Historically African American Leisure Destinations around Washington, D.C.* Charleston, SC: The History Press, 2015.

Kahrl, Andrew W. "New Negroes at the Beach: At Work and Play Outside the Black Metropolis." In *Escape from New York: The New Negro Renaissance Beyond Harlem,* by Davarian L. Baldwin and Minkah Makalani. Minneapolis: University of Minnesota Press, 2013, 335–57.

McMillian, Lewis K. "East Baltimore." *Afro American,* April 14, 1928, 6.

Vaz, Matthew. "'We Intend to Run It': Racial Politics, Illegal Gambling, and the Rise of Government Lotteries in the United States, 1960–1985." *Journal of American History* (June 2014): 71–96.

Chapter 3

Afro American. "Feminine Front: Sigma Gamma Rho Honors Marlene Thompson." July 5, 1969, 14.

———. "500 to Atlanta for Sorority Convention." August 30, 1969, 15.

———. "Mattie Coasey, Charter Member NCNW." February 14, 1981, 12.

———. "Mrs. Alleyne Secretary of Voters' Unit." November 14, 1953, 8.

———. "National Council Launches Drive for 500,000 Interracial Members." December 4, 1948, 11.

———. "Senate Fight Cost $3,000 in Fourth." December 18, 1954.

Austin, Finis. "Gibson's Army Attacks Linked to Repentance." *Afro American*, October 12, 1946, 7.

Crenson, Matthew A. *Baltimore: A Political History*. Baltimore, MD: Johns Hopkins University Press, 2017.

Hanson, Joyce A. *Mary McLeod Bethune & Black Women's Political Activism*. Columbia: University of Missouri, 2003, 124.

Marquardt, Tom. "Tragic Chapter of Crownsville State Hospital's Legacy: Crownsville State Hospital's Story Was One in Which African-Americans with Mental Illness Were Warehoused." *Capital Annapolis*, June 2, 2013, A1.

Smith, Elaine M. *Mary McLeod Bethune and the National Council of Negro Women: Pursuing a True and Unfettered Democracy*. Montgomery: Alabama State University, 2003, 62.

Stuckey, Zosha. "Race, Apology, and Public Memory at Maryland's Hospital for the 'Negro' Insane." *Disability Studies Quarterly* 37, no. 1 (2017).

Chapter 4

Adams, Victorine Q. "Provident Hospital: The Tearing Down of a Legacy." *Afro-American Red Star*, June 30, 2000, A9.

Jackson, Robert L. "A History of Provident Hospital, Baltimore, Maryland." *Journal of the National Medical Association* 59, no. 3 (May 1967): 157–65.

Morgan College Bulletin, January 1949, 34–40.

Sterne, Joseph R.L. "Integrating Delinquents Is Ruled Out." *Baltimore Sun*, January 13, 1956, 32.

Chapter 5

Afro American. "People, Places and Things." January 23, 1971, 5.

Avins, Miriam. "Green Spaces Boost Baltimore's Bottom Line." *Baltimore Sun*, June 1, 2016.

Baltimore Sun. "City Councilman Julian Dies at 61." December 3, 1978, 1.

Banisky, Sandy. "'Council' Victorine Adam to Forgo Reelection Bid." *Baltimore Sun*, July 2, 1983, C1.

3200 Carlisle Block Association. "Victorine Q. Adams Community Garden." www.3200carlisle.com/community-garden.

Additional Sources

Bible. Holman Christian Standard version.

Crenson, Matthew A. *Neighborhood Politics*. Cambridge, MA: Harvard University Press, 1983.

Davis, Cyprian. *The History of Black Catholics in the United States*. New York: Crossroad Publishing Company, 1990.

Gibson, Larry S. *Young Thurgood: The Making of a Supreme Court Justice*. Amherst, NY: Prometheus Books, 2012.

Giddings, Paula. *When and Where I Enter: The Impact of Black Women on Race and Sex in America*. New York: W. Bantam Books, 1984.

Neverdon-Morton, Cynthia. *Afro-American Women of the South and the Advancement of the Race, 1895–1925*. Knoxville: University of Tennessee Press, 1989.

Orr, Marion. *Black Social Capital: The Politics of School Reform in Baltimore, 1986–1998*. Lawrence: University Press of Kansas, 1999.

Shaw, Stephanie J. *What a Woman Ought to Be and Do: Black Professional Women Workers during the Jim Crow Era*. Chicago: University of Chicago Press, 1996.

INDEX

ABOUT THE AUTHOR

I da E. Jones is the university archivist at Morgan State University. She became intrigued with Victorine Adams during Morgan's sesquicentennial celebration in 2017. She concluded that the history of African American Baltimore and, to a large extent, Maryland have some kind of Morgan connection with organizations and individuals. She is a consummate scholar who believes deeply in the words of Mrs. Mary McLeod Bethune, who stated, "Power must walk hand in hand with humility and the intellect must have a soul."